Find Love Online

A 30 day journey to find love and life long happiness

Fiona Caddies-Miller &
Bjorn Miller

Copyright © 2013 Fiona Caddies & Bjorn Miller

All rights reserved.

ISBN: 0992419913

http://www.findloveonline.co

"A long journey with many lessons before we met. Now a new, longer and exciting journey together as one..."

with love, Fi & Bjorn

Contents

Introduction

Why did we write this book? 11
HOW FIND LOVE ONLINE CAN HELP YOU 13
OUR STORY 16

Step One: FIND YOUR TRUE SELF 25

Know your inner self - Why the 21 days? 26
Happiness and comfort within 28
Does fear hold you back? 34
Find comfort in your discomfort! 40
Let go 45
Self fulfilling prophecy 50
Laws of Attraction 55
Be magnetic! 59
What are you looking for? 64
The Clean Up! 65
Your Authentic Self 68

Step Two: ATTRACT THE RIGHT ROMANCE 76

Finding Romance 76
   Why and how are we doing this?......................78
   Why go online? 80
   Ways to find romance...84
Your Online Profile 91
   TIP 1: Honesty 91
   TIP 2: Overselling 94
   TIP 3: Confidence 95
   TIP 4: Key words 97
   TIP 5: What's important....................................100
   TIP 6: Negativity 102
   TIP 7: Entice with moderation 103
   TIP 8: Username and profile punchline 104
   TIP 9: Stand out but stay true 106
   TIP 10: Be tasteful..109
Your description..110
Which dating site is right for me? 113

Step Three: HOW TO PICK THE RIGHT ONE?.......119

   TIP 1 - How to pick a scammer and liar....................124

TIP 2 - Repeat relationships 129

TIP 3 – Signs to dodge or run away! 132

TIP 4 - Learn from your mistakes 145

TIP 5 – Your scars and your partner 146

TIP 6 – It's just not going to work 147

TIP 7: Criticism: reflection of the critic 153

TIP 8: A toxic relationship 154

TIP 9: How to say no to a second date..................... 157

TIP 10: Be 100% happy 159

Bonus! KEEPING YOUR ROMANCE ALIVE 163

TIP 1: Date nights 164

TIP 2: Communication.. 169

TIP 3: Honesty and Openness 170

TIP 4: Eliminate what you both dislike doing............ 172

TIP 5: Make it fair.. 172

TIP 6: Five positives for one negative 173

ABOUT US 175
CONTACT 178
REFERNCES.. 182
NOTES 184

Fi, today I marry you, my best friend, You are the one I laugh with, dream with, learn with and live for. I promise to love and care for you, and follow you wherever our journey leads us. I promise to love and cherish you and always do my best to be on time. But most of all, I promise to be a true friend and loyal husband to you. I love you, you are my one.

Bjorn, today I marry you, my best friend, You are the one I laugh with, dream with, learn with and live for. I promise to love and care for you, and follow you wherever our journey leads us. I promise to love and cherish you more than I do chocolate and ice cream. But most of all, I promise to be a true friend and loyal wife to you. I love you, you are my one.

These words marking our commitment to each other were the very first words for the new chapter in our lives. In fact they were the marker for Volume II in the lives of Fi & Bjorn. Our single lives (Volume I) were no longer.. a life of love, excitement, joy, happiness and commitment lies ahead!

Introduction

Why did we write this book?

Throughout this book, we'll share with you our personal struggles in relationships (as well as individual life discoveries) and what we've learnt along the way. We, and our friends, have collectively experienced some typical relationships which we're sure you'll be able to relate to.

We feel that by sharing with you what we've done, the good and the bad and how we managed to find each other, you'll be able to find your one and only!

We knew we had found it tough to find someone we felt the warm and fuzzies for, and not only that, for feelings to be reciprocated and long term!

Then we found each other online. We told our online company, eHarmony of our success and from there, media exposure flowed!

We were part of an eHarmony TV ad campaign that ran for well over six months. During this time newspapers wanted a love story as they said "everyone loves a good love story". We were asked by Channel 7 to go on their morning show, Weekend Sunrise, going to air to half a million people. Our thoughts again... everyone wants to find love, that companion, their happily ever after. We were also approached by magazines, again wanting to tell their readers about our love story, reaching millions of people.

Our thoughts were not of fame but "WOW, every single person wants to find love if all kinds of media want to tell our story!".

We thought a little more and realised, our friends have struggled to meet their lifelong partners too. We remember many a coffee or a beer with our besties consoling them and devising plans for ways to meet the right one for them. So now, it wasn't just the two of us, and it wasn't everyone else in this world, it was our immediate friends and families too. EVERYONE wants to find love and live happily ever after – the fairytale endings we've always known.

Now before you think this book is going to show you a quick fix for your happily ever after, think again. We believe you can live a happy and healthy existence with your one and only for a very long time but it takes work, positive work. Our belief is that all aspects of your life will involve work - so when you've reached perfection, it will be your time to leave this Earth. Life is a journey, always learning, always growing and in your relationships, together you learn and grow, always creating the life you want. You choose your happiness and existence.

Let's share our story and our approach to life.

HOW FIND LOVE ONLINE CAN HELP YOU

There are 3 sections to this book:

1st – We feel you need to look within yourself first before finding your "one". Otherwise, you're simply finding an object that you think you want  (possibly based on aesthetics or on what society leads you to believe you need). A little bit of soul searching goes a long way!

2nd – Your Partner – now that you know yourself better, we devise a plan (including worksheets) of how to find your true "one". Our main focus with this book will help you be successful online. This is how we did it and we believe it opens you up to people all over the world, rather than just in your 10km/mile radius. However, we will still briefly cover some other ideas so that you don't put all your eggs in one basket!

3rd – How to know your partner is the one

BONUS – a few hints and tips for how to maintain an amazing life and relationship together

OUR MISSION:

So... After years of just never meeting "the one", we finally found each other! Now it's your turn..

Our mission is to teach you the skills and the tools to finding your lifelong partner.. The bonus? You'll find that, along the way, you'll be happier in all aspects of your life.

A LITTLE POINTER FOR THIS BOOK:

We have written this book from our view of what works best. There are many ways to skin a cat so if our tips don't initially help you find your match, try again. Redo some of the questions but dig a little deeper. If this doesn't work, at least you will have learnt a lot more about yourself and you'll be well on your way to find the best path for you to meet your match!

We believe that this process takes time to allow you to put your best foot forward. The order of our book is designed to do this... So please don't skip to the last week.

In order to find love you need to love yourself first!

OUR STORY

In February 2011 we were first matched on eHarmony, an online dating website. We had both been searching for our "the One" for quite a while, not knowing how or when we would find the right person. After many failed relationships we both had decided to try online dating. We had heard so much about it, yet had no idea how a simple email would drastically change the rest of our lives.

Living in separate states of Australia, nearly 900km (560 miles) apart, Bjorn and I received each other's match on 12th February 2011. I thought, this guy looks friendly, I'll say hi so I sent him a "hello". Bjorn wrote me an email in reply almost immediately. From there, we wrote a couple of really long emails back and forth to each other! We then started chatting via gmail chat which went non-stop, all night for nights on end! At this time, Bjorn was living in Toowoomba and renovating a house. I was in Newcastle, running my own personal training business. With the daylight saving difference and my incredibly early work start times, I was getting 2-3hrs sleep a night as we would talk all night and into the early hours of the morning and I'd have to turn around to start work at 5am! Bjorn's deal wasn't much better, he was working hard labour for 12-14hrs each day on his house renovation. Needless to say, we obviously liked each other and the lack of sleep was worth it – we couldn't get enough of one another!

Our first date...

It had been 3 weeks since being matched and we'd both done our background checks on each other (of course, without the other knowing). We decided to meet in person. Our first date became a bit of a non-event. Bjorn drove from Toowoomba to Newcastle (approx. 9hrs). About 3hrs out of Newcastle, Bjorn ran in to some serious traffic! He was held up for an extra 3hrs with a car accident (kilometres of cars banked up!). Our fancy, "surprise location", romantic dinner had to be cancelled. At the time, I thought Bjorn was simply not that keen so wanted to step back a little. We caught up for coffee and lunch at a casual café the following day. With our nerves and personalities, Bjorn barely said a word and I talked non-stop. Our thoughts on each other were.. Fiona -

"WOW, he's really nice, VERY QUIET, sweet and beautiful hands. I'd like to see him again! He may not want to see me though as I was such a nervous chatterbox!" .. Bjorn – "WOW, she talks a lot! She's pretty but very small! I've always dated girls at least 5'9.. She comes up to my shoulder!.. I hope I can get used to this". Nerves and a bit of a rocky start, but there was obviously something there. Jetstar (a local airline) had some good travel deals on that weekend. We discussed this briefly on our date. Later that evening we spoke via text and agreed we liked each other and wanted to see if our meeting could go further and potentially be a relationship. The next day, we booked a 2 week holiday to Bali (for 3 months away). I guess we thought our relationship was more likely to move in the positive direction!!

The moment we realized we had something special...

Between meeting in March 2011 and going to Bali in June 2011, Bjorn moved back to Canberra and then to Sydney (I was still in Newcastle). Bjorn and I met in Sydney on weekends, staying in flashy hotels and eating out for each meal. As fun as this was, we didn't get to see each other in our home environments or meet each other's friends. In June, our Bali trip allowed us to spend 2 full weeks together, enough time to not be on "best behaviour". It was at this moment we knew we had something special. Simply being able to lie around silently with each other, being completely comfortable without the need to entertain each other, meant that our chemistry was more than "just dating". We wanted to open up to each other and potentially spend the rest of our lives together.

The engagement...

Bjorn and I travelled significantly the first year of our relationship – Brisbane, Melbourne, Sydney, Gold Coast, Bali, New York twice, Las Vegas, Utah to name a few. We spent quite a bit of money and took way too much time off work! So for 2012, we agreed, we wouldn't buy lavish presents for each other's birthday! Clearly, Bjorn didn't listen to this (unfortunately his birthday is BEFORE mine in the year). He had bought an engagement ring a month or so before my birthday. He tried to propose a few times but I kept ruining his plans (unknowingly of course). So, he decided about a week out from my birthday, he would propose on my actual birthday. This way, my birthday would put me off the engagement track (I had no idea anyway but Bjorn knows I'm pretty cluey, nosey and like to know what's going on so he needed a good plan). His plan

was amazing and wonderful! At this stage, I was still commuting weekly from Newcastle to Sydney. So I finished work that evening in Newcastle and raced down to Sydney. I said not to go to any trouble for dinner (on my birthday) as I'd be pretty late and not able to look pretty to go out. I arrived around 9pm in my ugg boots, tights and no makeup (and most likely partly sweaty/dirty hair too – it's my job to sweat!). Bjorn had candles all through the house, wine waiting and dinner cooking. There on the table waiting was a big bunch of a dozen roses and about 20 lilies! This was enough for me – a beautiful dinner and an amazing bunch of romantic flowers – remember, we weren't supposed to go to any trouble this year. I was already SO happy! Bjorn said "would you like your present now". I said "we agreed no presents"... he said "it's only small... wait there". He walked out towards me with a box which looked about the size of the boxes you get from the lingerie shops. Then when he handed it to me, it was heavy – I thought he was playing a trick on me and had weighed down a box full of some new underwear (as he's always telling me to stop wearing my old daggy undies and that I'm well overdue for new ones!). I was so wrong! I had wanted a new laptop so he went and bought exactly what I wanted – the brand new retina display MacBook Pro 15" with all the bells and whistles I could possibly want. This was well over what we'd agreed on! Then he said "there's one more small thing.. wait there and close your eyes". He ran away and came back and seemed to be squatting down in front of me (I couldn't really tell as my eyes were closed). I noticed that he seemed kind of nervous as he was sweating a little. I still didn't know what he was doing. I already had a really good present (great diversion!) and I still hadn't had any chocolate (my favourite food!). I thought he was going to put chocolate in my mouth with my eyes closed. He was hovering and stalling though, he kept pecking me on the lips. I started to screw my face up as I didn't know what Bjorn was doing – I thought he was going to put something awful in my mouth as a joke! Then Bjorn started laughing as I looked so funny and so far from the romantic, pretty look he was expecting to be proposing to. After all this, Bjorn popped the question and I was the happiest girl in the world! Of course I said yes. I jumped up and down with excitement – I was so excited, I got smile cramps in the back of my head! It was such a great night and such a great proposal! I was so excited to be marrying my perfect match!

Our wedding

I am a bit funny about numbers. I didn't want to get married in 2013 and we didn't want to be organizing a wedding for potentially 18 months so we decided to get married sooner rather than later! We set the date, never to happen again – 20.12.2012 – We cut the cake at 20:12 (8:12pm 24hr time). So we had a 20:12 20.12.2012 party! We searched high and low for a venue that truly reflected our personalities and us as a couple. We couldn't find anywhere we were happy with. We decided 6 weeks out from 20.12.2012, that we'd do the whole wedding ourselves at my mum's house. It was such a perfect day, a beautiful secret garden wedding – shabby chic style. We are so excited to build an amazing life together and experience life to the fullest!

FIND LOVE ONLINE

FIND YOUR TRUE SELF

*"Your beliefs become your thoughts,
Your thoughts become your words,
Your words become your actions,
Your actions become your habits,
Your habits become your values,
Your values become your destiny."
— Mahatma Gandhi*

Know your inner self - Why the 21 days?

We think that putting time aside to learn more about yourself and work out exactly what type of person you are is very important, so we have dedicated quite a bit of time for self discovery and reflection. You may want to rush through this part, however we have found the more you know about yourself the clearer it will be to find your perfect partner.

We have designed the next section to be completed thoroughly. Then over the next 21 days, we recommend you have a daily reflection and meditation (this should take you 10 minutes) to reset a positive outlook on life and yourself. It also takes 21 days to form a habit. So form a habit to start believing in yourself!

Remember... it's what you do most of the time that counts. So aim to set a routine where each day you spend 10 minutes reminding yourself of how amazing you are. Aim for 21 days straight and be as regular with this self-appointment as possible. If you miss a day.. well, that's ok. The aim is to do this for 21 days straight, then remind yourself throughout your life. The idea of the 21 days is that when a habit forms, which it should do after this time, it will become second nature to spend 10 minutes with just you, being present and giving yourself the gift of a little self love. Start each day well and watch your life change in a positive way!

"To love others you must first love yourself."
- Leo Buscaglia

This journey of self-discovery allows you project who you really are online and essentially attract more compatible matches.

I.e. Instead of having 'plenty of fish in the sea' but not one fish that interests you, you now have a pond full of awesome fish you want to meet – they're just like you!

Knowing yourself can be challenging. How well do you know what you like and what you don't? Odds are that there is something that is holding you back, especially when it comes to finding your perfect partner.

We are all different in our own way... and that is simply ok!

Coming up, we work through some questions with you to outline exactly what drives you, what you love, and what you don't like. Once you identify these areas you will find Step 2 much easier. You will find filling out your profile will be a breeze!

You may find that these lists change each time you do them, or else there are core elements that stay consistent.

You need to pick the most common or else the most passionate items to move forward.

Happiness and comfort within

What makes you buzz? What makes you glow?

A common mistake many people make is looking for a partner to make them happy. In actual fact you are the creator of your happiness. Our aim for you is to have your own inner happiness and comfort within. It's at this point you find that special person to share your true happiness and inner beauty.

> *Happiness doesn't depend on any external conditions, it is governed by our mental attitude. - Dale Carnegie*

To start with, let's get you to jot down 5 very simple points of what you love about yourself. Hint... you're not allowed to say nothing! Write down 5 points now!

What do I love about myself?

1) _____

2) _____

3) _____

4) _____

5) _____

Next let's move on to parts of you that you don't like. Are there any (you don't have to have any)? Write down the top 5 that come to mind.

What parts of myself do I not like?

1) _____

2) _____

3) _____

4) _____

5) _____

After you have answered this. Think about if these are behaviours or traits? i.e. Were you born like this?

Behaviours are a choice. You can change these behavioural patterns and habits instantly... just put your mind to it!

Meditations and visualization are two great tools to use here. Start seeing yourself in a positive light. Feed your positive dog and allow your inner furry friend to grow healthily and happily!

Here's a little visualization technique for you to help see how happy your true self really is!

Close your eyes and place your hands on your belly. Breathe into your hands.

Take yourself to the place where you felt...

HAPPINESS (where you were truly happy)

LOVE (where you knew you were unconditionally loved... you knew how special you were)

PASSION (a time when you were chasing a dream)

INNER CELEBRATION (when you finally achieved that goal or reached for that special something you really, really wanted!)

STEP ONE – FIND YOUR TRUE SELF

Now look back at those dislikes you had about yourself. When you feel this way, take yourself back to one or all of these visualization places to remind yourself of how special you are, breathe (take at least 10 deep breaths) and be calm. Nothing is as ever as bad as it seems. In time, reminding yourself of how special you are and being positive will take over your negative feelings towards yourself.

If some of these dislikes you wrote down were traits...

See if you can see yourself in another light. Why is this trait SO bad? Why can't it be seen as a gift? Play the cards you've been dealt and genuinely be happy with them. You have been made an individual for a reason. Why would it be so much better to look like someone else? Allow your inner beauty to shine through. After all, isn't that what you look for in others? Have you ever thought they are looking for the same thing in you? True friends and/or lovers only ever see your inner beauty. Your outfits, your possessions, your haircut, your makeup, your height, your weight, your skin type, (need I go on?) are either bonuses or simply the shell that carries you to your daily activities and allow you to simply live. If you currently judge people on these material things, have a think as to why? Is your judgment on others based on insecurity you have yourself? Be truly honest with yourself.

Your inner beauty, light, energy and vitality come from your self-beliefs and you display this through your positive behavior! Only you can decide how you view yourself. Focus on your strengths and teach yourself to view your traits (the ones you currently see as undesirable) as quirky or a specialty. Don't get me wrong; if a day at the spa makes you feel special, a new pair of fancy shoes or your brand new car gives you a little buzz, that's A-OK. It just doesn't make you who you are.

> *"There is only one way to happiness and that is to cease worrying about things which are beyond the power of our will."*
> *- Epictetus*

Both behaviours and traits can be changed. The question is do you want to? If you answered yes, then have a think about the reasoning behind this and use it as motivation for change!

"Happiness is not something ready made. It comes from your own actions."
Dalai Lama

Does fear hold you back?

You are after LOVE right? Finding the perfect partner? To really find your one, you need to look deeper within yourself. What is really holding you back? Often our fears are something we try not to think about. We see these fears as our flaws. More often than not, we've created our own story, forced ourselves to believe that something could only be or happen a certain way or perhaps  you've encountered a bad experience which has led you to believe you were not worthy or good enough in some way.

So, how do you identify your fears? Simply realizing your fears can be invigorating, empowering, life changing. Other times, you may need to do a little more work, on your own or by seeing a professional to help you work through these things. However you do it, at the time it may feel confronting but you'll be so glad you did! To know your fears and address them is power in itself (your inner power, not power over anyone else).

Ok, it's time to assess if anything is holding you back or stopping you from finding your ONE.

Do you keep meeting the same type of person over and over? Sometimes the person you are with can be a reflection of you or their behavior is a reflection of an issue you have not resolved within yourself. You simply push that bit of yourself aside as it's too hard to deal with. This is not always the case, sometimes the people we meet are not who we think they are and that's a whole other story. I'll leave this for you to work with your professional if it's a serious case.

Alternatively, do you choose that person you think others expect you to be with or you feel that's the type "I SHOULD" be with? Do you simply fear being true to yourself and finding that quirky, awesome match to your inner nerd because you have a belief that you're supposed to "be cool" instead of finding the amazing match to your bushwalking, bug-inspecting, inner nature-loving person because you think you're supposed to be a "city-slicker".

If you answered YES to either of these, I hope you find some benefit by the up and coming worksheet. If you don't relate to this, read on, your fear may not be based on expectation you put on yourself or related to previous relationships.

There are no rules.. The rules are: BE YOURSELF. Let your inner child shine through and attract what and who you truly love, not what you think you're supposed to. You know what? There is someone out there wanting to do exactly what you LOVE to do and wanting to LOVE exactly how you LOVE being.

Identifying and facing your fears can be one of the most challenging aspects to online love. Why is this? If you portray that person you think you're supposed to be? You will attract exactly that, over and over... and what's worse? That bug-loving bushwalker completely missed you. Your fears come from within, they are an emotion that can be overcome, but how do you overcome them? Don't stress, we have a little worksheet coming up. By overlooking these fears temporarily will create self-doubt and uncertainty or repeat, failing relationships. We certainly don't want that. So step up to the plate and work through this. You'll be so glad you did!

Fear is inbuilt to protect ourselves. One type of fear is natural and most people would agree. For example 10 lions surround you and there is no way out. You fear for your life. The other fear is more complex, something you create in your thoughts ("your story"), something that may not be logical to others. These fears could stem from a self-esteem issue or past experiences. For example you were picked on about having big feet, or a previous partner didn't treat you very well and you think it's going to happen again.

Facing your fears is the only true option, take them head on and see your life blossom! Feel a weight lifted off your shoulders. Watch all of your relationships change for the better!

By facing your inner fear, you will have the confidence to say what you want, say no and move on. Sometimes this alone is liberating! You'll no longer feel compelled to simply accept something because you're too scared to keep searching and pushing your limits to find what you actually REALLY want!

So how do you move forward? First step is identifying your fears. Sit down for a couple of minutes and list below the 5 fears that are stopping you from finding LOVE.

Some questions to prompt you to draw out your fears... What am I scared of (in relationships, in meeting people, in anything in your life... Alternatively, what do I hide from others? What part of you hasn't shone for a while because you haven't allowed it to due to fear of judgment)

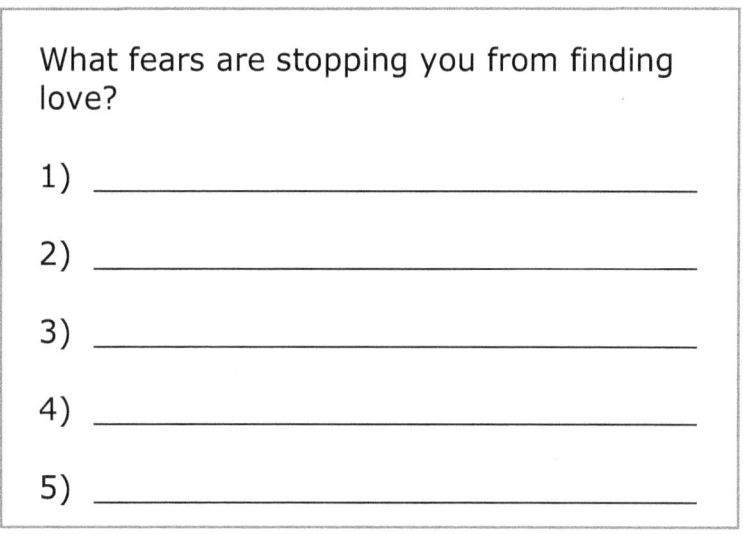

If I step into my fear, what's the worst that can happen? Is it really that bad? Really? Use this table:

My Fear (give it a title)	What is the worst that can happen if I step into my fear? What happens if I let go and be who I know I can be?	Is the worst that can happen that bad?

So you have identified your fears.

Why do you feel this way?

How can you overcome this feeling? More often than not it's doing that exact thing which you think is the worst thing that can possibly happen. E.g. You're scared to receive awards on stage; you don't want to walk across the stage in front of all those people! You fear completely face planting in front of a huge crowd. Possibly the biggest gift to you would be for what you fear to happen to you, bigger than you ever imagined! You're exposed and there's nothing you can do about it! Instead of being mortified and never stepping on a stage again, taking sickies or avoiding ever possibly being given an award, embrace it. Really think about it, was it that bad? Could you simply laugh it off and have a giggle with everyone else? Then realize you've overcome something that's been holding you back for far too long, you've conquered a fear, and the weight has been lifted!

Find comfort in your discomfort!

By practising stepping into your fears, you'll get better and better at this, to the point that you may even see it as a challenge and enjoy embracing and conquering your fears one by one. You're allowed to start small... no need to jump out of planes or anything just yet, unless you really want to!!

Throughout my life, I have slowingly stepped into my fear. It has taken me 30 years of practising this. I can finally say, I find it liberating!! I've pushed myself to do certain things, pressured myself SO MUCH to be perfect immediately and it just wasn't fun at all. I hated it!

It was an accidental "stepping into my fear" that had me turn the corner and finally understand and love facing my fears!

I have Keenan Crisp (POWER LIVING MANLY) to thank for this...

I signed up to do my yoga teaching course. It was fabulous until I had to show my own self love and expression, through teaching, to a group that I didn't know at all.

What would they think of me? What if I stuff up? What if it's not what they want?

I burst into tears in front of a group of strangers and cried uncontrollably as Keenan kept pushing me, asking me why I was really crying. No one had ever done that to me before (and I doubt, even if I needed it to happen again, it would actually ever happen). Most people, even in learning situations like this, won't push people to do this as they will feel your pain and shy away from it for you. Keenan had the strength to recognize and push me to exactly where I needed to be. I didn't get to sit down, splash water on my face, do anything… I literally had to teach and he pushed me to teach from the heart. This was all being recorded on video (to make the whole experience even more amazingly mortifying… as I, at the time, felt).

After this whole 5-10mins of hell (as I felt) finished, I was horrified at how I responded to such a simple task. I took a good hard look at my inner self and the situation and assessed why it happened. I realized that I always pressured myself to be perfect, to never fail. I never showed anyone how I really felt. I was that person who crumbled in exams and hated being given a score based on someone's opinion.

Do you know what actually happened after my 10mins of hell? Absolutely nothing! A few people felt my pain of pressuring myself (I saw it in their faces) and not one person said a thing. I survived and I learnt some really valuable things about myself.

As humiliating an idea (of facing your fear) may seem, it's well worth doing… What's the worst that can happen? If you think you can survive the worst, and I can 99% assure you that what you think is the worst is probably actually about a tenth of what you think it is, then step up to the plate and LEARN & GROW from it!

My big lesson: I was limiting myself from fear of looking stupid or not being good enough. You have limitless possibilities and potential in life if you don't let fear hold you back!

The way I see it now is... everyone is his or her own biggest critic. We need to cut ourselves some slack sometimes. See ourselves how our best friend or our dearest pet would see us.

From finishing my yoga teaching course, I went on to teach yoga for the next 2.5yrs before closing my Personal Training, Nutrition Coaching and Yoga business to move to another city. The people who were the saddest were my yoga students. I had shared my own lessons with them, expressed myself and let them see me as a human being... From this, they could connect with me and implement these tools in their own lives. The beauty of yoga is, you open your body and mind up and learn so much in the process!

Without these limiting fears and now having your newfound inner strength allows you to put yourself out there, no matter what the situation, and have you finding the one for you, sooner!

So face your inner fear, have the strength to say what you want, say no when you need to and move on. Don't be owned by your story. Change your story!

Next we want you to list some things you would really like to give a go. Things that you have always wanted to do and had some fear or reason of why you haven't done it yet. What comes to mind straight away?

What would you like to give a go?	What is stopping you from doing them?	How are you going to overcome them?

It may not be as simple as 1,2,3... You may have to just push the boundaries a little and keep learning from each experience. The main thing is... move! If you move, you have a chance to grow.

If you're frozen by fear, you cannot move forward.

Sometimes you make mistakes and temporarily take a step back but at least you know not to do it again. It's better to have tested it out than always wondering what could have been.

Be not afraid of going slowly, be afraid only of standing still.
- Chinese Proverb

Let go

"The truth is, unless you let go, unless you forgive yourself, unless you forgive the situation, unless you realize that the situation is over, you cannot move forward." — Steve Maraboli

Life doesn't happen to you, it happens through you! When you force situations to be how you think they should be, not so grand things happen... and then you feel they happen TO you. Your new positive beliefs and behaviours will lead you in the direction to have your life simply happen!! The bigger picture? LIFE HAPPENS THROUGH YOU! So spread life and vitality, go and LIVE! Be in the present moment, LET GO of the past, LET GO of how you think the future should be and simply be. Change the way you constantly critique and force your life. Be present, LET GO, breathe, be free and make this wonderful life you were given happen. Watch your friendships change, the way see you see the world change and see the positive ripple effect from your new way of being. Letting go is freedom, your life will blossom and LIFE HAPPENS THROUGH YOU!

When you try to force life to move in the direction you

think it should, you set yourself up for failure and disappointment. By simply trusting your gut, "going with the flow" and letting go of the should-be-happenings, you allow life to take you on a journey.

You have more than one road to your destination, your final resting point. Our destiny leads us in the direction we're meant to go but this doesn't mean it's always going to be fabulous. Sometimes we have life lessons to learn so whatever happens, it was meant to happen. If everything was amazingly great, you wouldn't know it, it would just be normal to you. You need to have a bumpy ride, a few hiccoughs along the way to appreciate greatness! This applies to all aspects of your life, most definitely the relationships you have along the way and even within the relationship you'll find with "your one".

LET GO, LIVE LIFE, LOVE LIFE, LEARN FROM LIFE

STEP ONE – FIND YOUR TRUE SELF

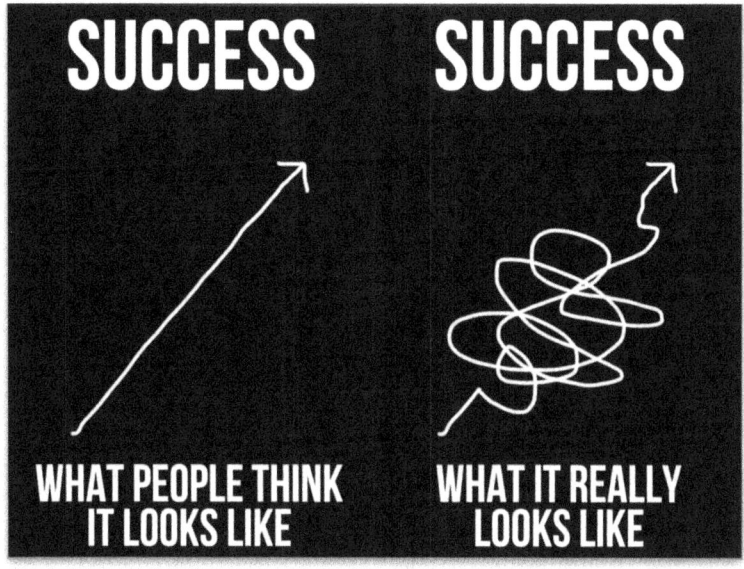

SUCCESS, YOUR LIFE, YOUR RELATIONSHIPS

Between two pains comes pleasure, between two pleasures comes pain

"We may lay it down that Pleasure is a movement, a movement by which the soul as a whole is consciously brought into its normal state of being; and that Pain is the opposite." - Aristotle's Rhetoric

These two emotions are on opposite ends of the spectrum with contentment in the middle or simply a feeling of being normal. We simply cannot have one without the other. We will always be drawn to pleasure and want to be as far away from pain as possible, but we need to experience this push-pull concept to experience life. Know that we're supposed to experience all emotions. The key is to not hold on to them. Experience and let them go. Remember... BE PRESENT. Be in the present moment with no attachments and use all these experiences, good or bad, to your advantage for an amazing life!

> *"Letting go doesn't mean that you don't care about someone anymore. It's just realizing that the only person you really have control over is yourself."* - Deborah Reber

Let go... don't hold on to life so tightly that you forget to live... to live and feel pleasure... to live and feel pain. Remember that... between each pair of emotions (the positive and negative), lies contentment. However much we will not devote our lives to reaching contentment, like monks do (the average Western population), we can reach for a modified version. We can learn from the crazy highs and lows we experience as kids and teenagers and then continue as we grow older and experience more things in life. Each stage in our life will have us learn different things, all of which we are meant to learn. The more times we experience these emotions, the highs and lows will not be as dramatic as we know what to expect and how to deal with them. They will be more like little ripples in a lake rather than the tsunami / drought and rollercoaster experiences we once had. This is not to say we can't enjoy ourselves. I feel the more we learn, the more we can live and experience life so go for it! Let go and let it flow! Everything happens for a reason :)

Next, let's list what you need to let go of, and what is the worst thing that can happen if you do? E.g. Self doubt, insecurities, everyone is out to get you...

What do you need to let go of?	What is the worst that can happen if you let go?

Self fulfilling prophecy

What you think and expect, you become.

Negative thoughts, draw negative people towards you and make negative things keep happening. You expect and believe all people are therefore like this.

Conversely, positivity makes and attracts more positivity. Positive things keep happening. You believe all people are positive like you and life is simply like this.

Choose what you would like. If it really tickles your fancy being negative and you get a kick out of disagreements and nastiness then be that way. More than likely the one you end up with enjoys this way of being too.

Should you feel that being positive and being surrounded by positivity feels right for you, then choose this path. My personal choice will always be to choose the positive path. For some happiness doesn't always equal positivity. Either way,

Always believe something wonderful is going to happen..

do what makes YOU happy and know that you will attract exactly what you project and believe is going to happen.

Whatever we expect with confidence becomes our own self-fulfilling prophecy - Brian Tracy

Do one thing each day that brings joy into your life. Spread this joy and receive it back.

What makes you truly happy?

What can you do which will bring this true happiness into your daily life?

It's so cliché, but I just love sunrises and sunsets! I love the sun shining and I'm addicted to seeing parts of nature in various times of the day. If I don't do this, I feel a little lost. My phone is full of basically the same photos – the amazing afternoon sun over the ocean, waves, pretty sunlight through the trees, nature, my beautiful cat... you get the picture. I also love going for a jog and seeing people run with their dogs. The dogs seem to smile then look at their owners with unconditionally loving eyes. The happiness I feel in these moments, takes the harshness of life away from my thoughts and I see the world through soft eyes. It's from this place that I share my love with my husband. Take these moments and have your positivity outweigh your negativity.

Whilst ever you believe you're doomed or you're not worthy, you are. Whilst ever you expect that all men/women will be (insert your negative expectation of potential partner), they will be, time and time again. Your preconceived ideas and beliefs have attracted exactly that.

Believe and expect greatness and happiness. Remind yourself daily of what an amazing life exists out there for you; for what you already have and what you will have, personally and in a partner...

So write down one thing (or more if you like) that makes you happy!

What makes you happy?

1) _____

2) _____

3) _____

4) _____

5) _____

Choose one thing to do each day. Make sure you do it and see your life change and move in a positive direction.

If you're stuck for ideas or you're quite down in the dumps and you simply cannot think of one thing that makes you happy... here are a few tips...

Ask some friends what makes them happy – ask them to

list their "one" thing.

Try some of their things... after all, they're your friends, you may like doing the same thing!

Write a grateful log – Write down things you're grateful for, even if they haven't happened yet (this is the beginning to your manifestation).

> *"When you are grateful, fear disappears and abundance appears." – Anthony Robbins*

Go outside, stick your feet in the dirt or the sand and create some physical grounding. In yoga and the spiritual world, this is seen as nourishing your root chakra. Essentially you will feel more grounded.

Do yoga! Test out the various styles! There are so many! Here's a list of some common styles, do some research and see what suits you:

- Bikram

- Hatha

- Vinyasa

- Ashtanga

- Iyengar

- Restorative

You could also try meditation. If this interests you Google Deepak Chopra's 21-day Meditation Challenge.

Finding peace and calm in your life may give you the space to see where and how you find joy.

Remember what you think, believe, perceive and expect will be your self fulfilling prophecy.

Laws of Attraction

This is the name given to the belief "like attracts like" and that by focusing on positive or negative thoughts, one can bring about positive or negative results.

In the spiritual and yoga world, this is often referred to as manifestation. I have some worksheets and manifestation practice examples for you below.

There have been many studies on brain activity to show contagious behaviour and each time there is proof that it does happen. It appears our brain reads others' actions as if we are doing exactly that. Conversely, our actions cause similar action-representations in the brains of others.

In saying this, if you find happiness and interest in someone's actions and behaviours, you'll most likely want to join them and do the same. So, if you are being your best self, you will attract exactly that! You'll attract someone to share your loves, enjoy life with you and have a colourful, exciting existence. Remember all the tips from our journey together so far, start projecting who you really are and believe in yourself. Get out there, live life to the fullest and you'll find your match!

On the flip side, as I have said before, if you are negative, always sitting in your comfort zone or simply being a bit blah, you will attract much of the same. If you want someone to be like that with you, then that's great, stay the way you are. Couch potatoes unite!

The law of attraction – like attracts like

Manifestation – see what connects with you. You may like to do all of these!

MEDITATION

> **Deepak Chopra's Guided Mediation**
> Free and paid for guided meditation. High quality audio downloads.
> http://www.chopra.com/community/online-library/guided-meditations
>
> **Meditation Oasis**
> Offering free guided meditation via Website, iTunes and iPhone app.
> http://www.meditationoasis.com/podcast/listen-to-podcast/
>
> **Blissitations**
> Guided meditations, visualizations, affirmations and other goodness.
> http://www.entheos.com/blissitations
>
> **My Thought Coach**
> Free meditations on a broad range of topics.

STEP ONE – FIND YOUR TRUE SELF

http://www.mythoughtcoach.com/LibraryPage.aspx

DREAM BOARDS

O Dream Board: Envision Your Best Life™
Oprah offers one of the best online dream boards around.
http://www.oprah.com/spirit/O-Dream-Board-Envision-Your-Best-LifeTM

Vision Board
This dream board offers a complete creation package for free. Lot's of bells and whistles here.
http://www.visionboardsite.com/

Map our lives
Offering lots of dream board and goal setting options.
http://www.mapourlives.com/

INTENTIONS

Set Your Goals
A good resource that explains how to set and achieve your goals.
http://www.goal-setting-motivation.com/set-your-goals/how-to-set-goals/

Stickk
A unique approach to goal setting, including options to add support from friends.
http://www.stickk.com/

LifeTick
A paid goal setting application. Very comprehensive site with tons of features.
http://lifetick.com/

GRATEFUL LOG

Gratitude Log
The happiest place on the internet!
http://www.gratitudelog.com/

The Power Of Gratitude
Have a listen to Michael Losier talk about showing gratitude, appreciation and love on Oprah Radio.
http://www.oprah.com/oprahradio/The-Power-of-Gratitude

Write your own log!
Put pen to paper and write your own Grateful Log! List what you are already grateful for. You could also try listing things you plan to be grateful for - as if they have already happened... helping you to start believing!

Be magnetic!

It comes down to your mindset!

You know those people whom everyone just loves, you can't help but love them too and you just want to be them? They seem to effortlessly draw people to them and seem to be surrounded by love and goodness… Well, you can have that too!

It's your mindset! As I said previously in the self fulfilling prophecy section, what you think, believe, perceive and expect will be your self fulfilling prophecy. If you examined those amazingly magnetic people, you wouldn't find they had exact physical features, the same hair length or colour or be a certain height. You would find they have a similar approach to life, a way of being. They are content and grateful simply being.

The whole purpose of these first 21 days is for you to realize your full potential and see yourself as you did when you were a young child, free of self criticism, negativity and the effects of society. You were happy being you and you appreciated every moment. You were living in the present moment, not worrying about the future or fretting about the past.

It's not what you have or your latest outfit that draws people to you. It's the quality of being in touch with your inner self, being centered. When you are internally strong yet peaceful, aligned but free, people are drawn to you. There is an inbuilt mechanism inside of us that always wants to bring us back to our natural state. We are born balanced, strong and stress-free. We are all attracted to this, as it's how we all ultimately would like to be. How easily we forget and allow external influences to create imbalances within us.

It's time to change things around, focus on your breath and being in the now (present), create a sense of peace and calm in your life. By simply being, your true self will shine through. Your untouchable self-belief will make you one of those magnetic people. There is a confidence within you, not confidence that screams arrogance or narcissism, confidence that shows your strength. We all want that deep confidence and we're drawn to it.

Meditation, Qi Gong (including Tai Chi) and Restorative Yoga are very good ways to help you connect with your breath and being present. Setting time aside to do one or some of these practices can make such a huge difference to your mindset and way of life.

Gratitude is another way of being which makes people simply want to surround you. By being grateful for what you have, neither needing nor wanting anything, appreciating all that surrounds us simply frees us to see the world positively. It doesn't take much for negative people to rub off on us, nor does it positive. With so many awful things happening in the world, when people come across positivity and with gratitude, they simply want more. When you are so grateful for what life is presenting you, people want to absorb your gratitude. So love yourself, love what you have, big or small, love those around you, and be grateful and magnetic.

Making some positive changes to your life will kick start this magnetic process. Regardless, if you want to build friendships or meet your life partner, your behaviour and approach to life will determine who you attract.

You should feel beautiful and you should feel safe. What you surround yourself with should bring you peace of mind and peace of spirit. - Stacy London

"You are the average of the 5 people you spend most of your time with." – Jim Rohn

This applies to all aspects of life... positivity, lifestyle, financial status.

*Surround yourself with only people who are going to lift you higher.
- Oprah Winfrey*

Let's list what you're already grateful for and what you will be grateful for (which you know is coming your way).

What are you grateful for - now and into the future?

1) _____

2) _____

3) _____

4) _____

5) _____

6) _____

7) _____

8) _____

9) _____

10) _____

STEP ONE – FIND YOUR TRUE SELF

Next, who will you surround yourself with to keep lifting your spirits higher? Remember... You are the average of the 5 people you spend the most time with!

Who will you surround yourself with to make you soar?

1) _____

2) _____

3) _____

4) _____

5) _____

What are you looking for?

If you're looking for someone to make you happy, think again. Being happy within yourself will draw someone toward you who is also happy within themselves. It is at this point you can join together and be synergistically happy. It is a recipe for disaster if you are looking for someone to mask your own pain and suffering. It may temporarily work for you but then the relationship will slowly fall apart at the seams and the cycle begins.

Look within, accept you for you, be content and draw that amazing person toward you.

The Clean Up!

Now that you're happy within, it's time to clean up! Cleanse all aspects of your life.

Surround yourself with people who inspire you and make you feel great. Remember…

> *"You are the average of the five people you spend the most time with." — Jim Rohn*

Now…

Get rid of the people (or at least limit your exposure, sometimes we cannot simply avoid those we prefer not to be around) who are negative, put you down or bring you down.

Limit exposure to negativity in your workplace.

Who should I limit exposure to?	How can I achieve this?

Here are some great reads for how to cleanse your life for a positive existence. Altogether they cost around $30... so not a huge outlay for such an important life change.

Zen and the Art of Happiness

A pragmatic approach to cultivating a mindset of happiness so nothing can bring you down.
http://amzn.to/1a260dg

Boundaries: When to Say Yes, How to Say No to Take Control of Your Life

If you are Christian, this book is a top read explaining how

to set reasonable boundaries in order to follow the true path of spirituality. Includes real life stories!
http://amzn.to/17Sdwup

The Four Agreements: A Practical Guide to Personal Freedom
An inspiring book with many great lessons. Having sold over 5 million copies, this book is a must read!
http://amzn.to/1a2adh4

Your Authentic Self

For all we have travelled through in this section, I hope you can now see your true self, your authentic self and want to only ever show this self again! Here are some inspiring quotes for you. Believe it. Love it. Be it.

"The privilege of a lifetime is to become who you truly are."
- C.G. Jung

"The authentic self is soul made visible"
- Sarah Ban Breathnach

STEP ONE – FIND YOUR TRUE SELF

"Make a pact with yourself today to not be defined by your past. Sometimes the greatest thing to come out of all your hard work isn't what you get for it, but what you become for it. Shake things up today! Be You…Be Free…Share." - Steve Maraboli

"We have to dare to be ourselves, however frightening or strange that self may prove to be." - May Sarton

Only the truth of who you are, if realized, will set you free.
- Eckhart Tolle

If any man seeks for greatness, let him forget greatness and ask for truth, and he will find both.
- Horace Mann

Below are a few extra quotes and tips to keep you boosted and inspired! Before I leave you to complete your 21 days, let me remind you to really DO the WHOLE 21 DAYS! Take the time to form the habit of giving to yourself and loving yourself, just 10 minutes a day. Scan over your positive exercises in this step and do whatever resonates with you. Connect with yourself and be present (meditation, yoga and alike) daily for 21 days. If all you do is review your notes and picture yourself in a positive light (even simply 5 minutes a day, however 10 would be better!), you'll already be streets ahead!

NOW GO FOR IT!!

STEP ONE – FIND YOUR TRUE SELF

PROMISE YOURSELF

To be so strong that nothing can disturb your peace of mind.
To talk health, happiness and prosperity to every person you meet. To make all your friends feel that there is something in them.
To look at the sunny side of everything and make your optimism come true.
To think only of the best, to work only for the best, and to expect only the best.
To be just as enthusiastic about the success of others as you are about your own.
To forget the mistakes of the past and press on to the greater achievements of the future.
To wear a cheerful countenance at all timed and give every living creature you meet a smile.
To give so much time to the improvement of yourself that you have no time to criticise others.
To be too large for worry, too noble for anger, too strong for fear; and too happy to permit the presence of trouble.
To think well of yourself and to proclaim this fact to the world, not in loud words but in great deeds.
To live in the faith that the whole world is on your side so long as you are true to the best that is in you.

- Christian D. Larson 1912

30 things to do before you die:
Featured on Mind Body Green by Shannon Kaiser

1. Stop worrying about debt.
2. Forgive your ex-lovers.
3. Stop trying to control your outcome.
4. Look in the mirror and love yourself unconditionally.
5. Leave the job you hate.
6. Find your purpose and live it full heartedly.
7. Adopt a furry friend.
8. Don't feel guilty for holiday weight gain.
9. Trust that everything is in right order.
10. Travel to the place you keep thinking about.
11. Try something that scares you daily.
12. Be open to change.
13. Let go of your past.
14. Stop trying to change people.
15. Stop looking for answer outside of yourself.
16. Stop thinking you did something wrong.
17. Be your weird, crazy, beautiful self.
18. Follow your heart.
19. Risk everything for love.
20. Reject rejection.
21. See the world as a beautiful, safe, and loving place.
22. See everyone as equals.
23. Give up all attachments to stuff.
24. Recognize the journey is the reward.
25. Stay hopeful and optimistic in difficult situations.
26. Welcome all life lessons.

27. See the opportunities in every challenge rather than give up.
28. Live your values.
29. Inspire others by your own bigness.
30. Play with the world.

"Live life fully while you're here. Experience everything. Take care of yourself and your friends. Have fun, be crazy, be weird. Go out and screw up! You're going to anyway, so you might as well enjoy the process. Take the opportunity to learn from your mistakes: find the cause of your problem and eliminate it. Don't try to be perfect; just be an excellent example of being human."
- Tony Robbins

ATTRACT THE RIGHT ROMANTIC PARTNER
Your Profile

FINDING ROMANCE

Now this section should be relatively easy since you have spent some time on rediscovering your true self as well as now knowing what you want and don't want. Essentially, filling in your online profile should only take a few hours. From there you will need the extra 3 days to review and refine how you are presenting yourself. Sometimes when we write something, in our head, it sounds completely different from how it's actually being received. So fill in your profile the best you can. Then, as you receive matches and people connect with you, see if you see a pattern or if your matches are saying things that seem a little odd. Regardless of if you find anything or not, each day, re-read your profile as if you are your potential partner. Do you read like you are the person you know you are? Make those minor changes... be particular! Those small changes could be the difference between someone amazing contacting you or not.

Think of your profile as a mini assignment or you are submitting a tender. Would you put up something you only read once or twice? Or would you try your hardest to put the best darn assignment forward possible? Go for your own A+, not just a pass. Stand out and be proud!

Why and how are we doing this?

How did you go answering your "you" questions? Are you ready to meet "the one"? Have you spent the past 21 days reminding yourself how amazing and worthy you are? Are you rid of your checklist of the expectations you put upon yourself? I truly hope you have a new lease on life and feel positive about this next chapter in your life. After rediscovering all the great things about your true self and pushing aside everything that has been holding you back, filling out your profile will now be a breeze. You've done all the hard work. Now it's time to show the world who you really are and attract someone who sees the tip top person which you already know!

So are you ready to put yourself out there?

Honestly, we will never be 100% ready to do anything. If it scares you a little, all the more reason to step into your fear and embrace it! Accepting that nothing is ever perfect (and if it was, it would be oh so boring!!), timing will never be perfect and you, along with everyone else, will not be perfect either, will allow you to get out there and find your one sooner than you think. Waiting for perfection or the perfect moment will leave you always waiting. Then one day, you'll wake up and see all those years have passed by and you missed it, you lived without ever really living. Regardless of age or where you are in your life, the time is now. You cannot change the past or the future so start living now. What do you have to lose?

Accepting that you are born perfect, exactly how you were meant to be born, is your biggest gift and will allow you to step into your light. Your behaviours and self-limiting beliefs (as I'm sure you're now aware) are what make you less than perfect. You are exactly where you need to be right now, which is perfect for you right now. Perfection is your perception.

> *Nothing is perfect. Life is messy. Relationships are complex. Outcomes are uncertain. People are irrational.*
> *- Hugh Mackay*

Focus on you, your behavior and your true self. You cannot change anyone else but you.

> *"The reason many people in our society are miserable, sick, and highly stressed is because of an unhealthy attachment to things they have no control over."*
> *- Steve Maraboli*

Should you meet someone who definitely isn't your lifelong partner (and of course, there will be more of these than not, as we only need to find that one in the end!), evaluate and assess your experience for what it really is. Do not blame that person or yourself for them not being what you wanted them to be. If that person is not the nicest in their behavior, for whatever the reason, learn from your meeting. If you simply cannot learn anything from that person, I mean absolutely nothing, there are two things you can take from this encounter. Perhaps you were put into that meeting to inspire that person? You are their guardian angel, leading a change in their life direction. What do you get out of this? You've helped someone! Secondly, you can add this encounter to your warning bells list and someone who you wouldn't want to bring in to your life as he or she would prove to be too toxic. He or she is not what you're after and be happy that you can now recognize that.

Why go online?

Now this can be taken two ways. Regardless of your IQ, I feel, particularly in this fast-paced society, going online to find your partner is the smartest way to do things. In saying this, many people I know who have gone online have been intelligent people. Often, the more intelligent the person, the more likely they are to be in a higher-paid job. As we also know, a high paying job also often means long hours and even working at home. These people often don't have time, nor do they want to frequent bars and clubs. It also goes without saying, usually as we grow older we are wiser and looking for something deeper in our chosen relationship and we are also in higher-powered jobs requiring more of our brain space. So I could also say, wiser, not just smarter, people go online to find a deep and meaningful relationship which also means they are happy to search the globe rather than just their local pub. So regardless of your age, IQ or wanting someone quite specific, you are very wise to be searching for your lifelong partner online.

Smarter people go online
– Bjorn Miller

Some of the best things about going online are that:

You have instant depth and possible connection with your prospective partner, that isn't entirely physical! - You have a chance to go deeper to see their true self rather than at the level of a drunken meeting in a bar

You easily have differentiation between sex and love – this is a biggy for me! By checking out and choosing the right dating site for you, this will allow you to immediately narrow your pool to almost all relationship-only people. From this point, simply reading the profiles of your prospective partners allows you to determine what kind of love these prospectives are after. As this book is about love, I'm promoting the relationship side of things, however if you are reading this book and you're after only sex, then choose the right site and make it very clear about what you want on your profile. After all, do you really want to break someone's heart or at worst, have the hassle of dealing with the fallout when all you wanted was a shallow kind of relationship?

The world is your oyster! You have more choice, a bigger pool (and that pool is littered with like minded people, people you would actually considered speaking to again!)

The process is so easy! Once you have your profile up and you have determined what you're after, you can simply look at a few people on a daily or weekly basis, have a chat with whom you choose and unemotionally determine if they are worth considering for a relationship or not. Just as easily as you get talking to someone, you can cease talking to them should you choose. As I said before, you have a much higher chance of finding someone you actually share interests with versus being out and about and seeing who catches your eye then hoping you have something in common.

There is safety – provided you are careful about what you share and are sensible about who you choose to meet, online dating is fairly safe. Of course there will always be less than trustworthy people wherever you go. My meaning of safety with being online is that you have a buffer between meeting a total stranger and then suddenly going home with them or being in a relationship with them. Online dating allows you to really check people out from a distance whilst staying in the comfort of your own home. You have the time to analyse the situation, get to know someone on a deeper level, all before meeting in person. I recommend taking things very slowly and building trust between the two of you. We have more tips coming in Step 3!

It is easier than conventional dating, just one click away! It takes out the nerve-racking experience of walking up to a random in the street or a bar – what a bonus! You can be more confident online as you have had time to write and rewrite your profile ensuring you project yourself as how you want to be seen. We've all had moments of having major fumbling and stumbling when meeting someone we'd really like to impress! As I have said before, you can tailor your pool to match what you're looking for – to the finest of details!

Ways to find romance

I'm not going to go into a huge amount of detail here, as all methods of finding love are not the focus of this book. Finding love online is our key focus. I would like to just refresh your thinking brain to tap into all sides of you, what you used to do, what you miss and what you love doing. All these things are possible ways to meet people and are also certainly worth mentioning in your profile.

Your everyday life is a key indicator for who and what you should be looking for. If some of the things below are not current in your life but you would like them to be, they still count for the purpose of this exercise. What are your hobbies, interests, groups you are a part of or would like to be a part of?

Did many things come to mind from answering those couple of questions above? You can see there are many ways to find love and there are many hints and tips out there for finding love. Before we get into what these hints and tips are, I thought I would give you a short list of books that you may find helpful. If you need extra help, then read one or all of these books.

What is your WHAT?
Revealing a proven process for cultivating a life of purpose, conviction, and contribution by identifying and creating a

plan of action for bringing the ONE thing you were born to do to fruition.

http://amzn.to/IHT2vD

Love Smart: Find the One You Want--Fix the One You Got
Dr Phildoes a great job to explain how to be who you are and make you feel better about it.

http://amzn.to/1asQ8k6

Men Are from Mars, Women Are from Venus: The Classic Guide to Understanding the Opposite Sex
The classic guide to understanding the opposite sex.

http://amzn.to/18WmmIm

Here are some other ideas for you to find love and romance:

Since you're actually reading this book, I'm sure you've tried a few of these avenues you're about to list below and you haven't been as successful as you would have like so now you're looking for more options.

It is still worth reviewing the simple and obvious activities and interests in your life and keeping your options open. After all, with a new mindset, you just never know, someone may fall in your lap. In saying this, by simply filling in your profile, you've committed to putting it out there that you want a relationship, you're putting yourself out there in general and to be emotionally available. This act alone is like a switch inside of you. Your awareness changes, your mindset changes and you're ready to be open to potential partners. Being emotionally available will simply have you attracting more people. I speak about emotional availability in Part 3. If you think about it this way – once you have decided that you want a buy a car, you've decided on the colour, the type, the year and the release. Suddenly they're everywhere! You can't stop seeing them! Prior to this decision, you had barely noticed even one driving around. The same thing goes with your mindset, openness and decision that you're ready to meet your potential partner and also, you're truly happy being you. It's at this moment when many potential partners pop up, everywhere! So no more dwelling in the past, feeling sorry for yourself or thinking your relationship journey is a lost cause. The past 21 days should have proven to you how amazing you are and that you're ready to commit to change, commit to the openness that there are many amazing possibilities out there for you.

Keep your options open. Your online profile in your cyber world life may just be an inner belief catalyst to finding love out in the real world.

Every moment is an opportunity...

> *Your big opportunity may be right where you are now.*
> *- Napoleon Hill*

Hobbies and Interests:

As I mentioned earlier, knowing what your interests and hobbies are will help you in writing your profile. Let's get straight to it. Write down what you're truly interested in. Do it now :)

What are in my dreams? E.g. Overseas travel? Lazing on a beach? Jumping out of a plane? Finishing a marathon?

1) _____

2) _____

3) _____

4) _____

5) _____

What is it that you've always dreamed of doing and you haven't tried it yet? Write down at least 5 things.

> What are my interests? E.g. Books? Movies? TV? Coffee with friends?
>
> 1) _____
>
> 2) _____
>
> 3) _____
>
> 4) _____
>
> 5) _____

So, here are some ideas of where you may also meet people, have the **opportunity** or **openness** to meet people or simply possible ideas for where you can go for your dates with those you have met online.

Local activities and groups:

Build a network in your area. Is there a running group you want to join? Somewhere which has a community garden? The local Surf Club? In most towns and suburbs there are community boards near supermarkets or community centres etc.

A great online community board replacement is http://www.meetup.com/find/ - On here, you'll find so many different groups who meet up occasionally or quite regularly. There's basically everything you could think of on there... and if not, start a group!

Join a local sports team – Group sports can be a great way to meet like-minded people. Have a look around your local suburb, there's bound to be something on if sport is your thing.

Find somewhere to volunteer –helping others is a great way to meet new people and is good karma also ☺

If you are religious, there are lot's of opportunities to meet new people at your local church, mosque, temple or the like. See what social activities you can join in on.

Other places to meet people:

Your work environment is a great place to meet people. Try and speak to new people at a morning tea event, or if you are one to shy away from after work drinks – go along, push yourself and try something out of your comfort zone!

Your living situation; Do you live with housemates? Do they have friends or social outings? Tag along and try a different group of people. You never know what you may find ☺

Talk to your family. See if they have any social activities organized. Sometimes people could turn up where you least expect them to.

Do you have kids? If so, see if you can meet other single parents when picking them up or other related activities.

You could even join the Parent-Teacher Association?

The Bottom Line: Basically, get out of the house and experience life. You don't have to go out clubbing by yourself, just simply head out to various locations and places (whatever you've dreamed of) and shake up your routine a little.

Again, remember manifestation and law of attraction. You are and attract what you think, believe, perceive and put out to the rest of the world.

Your Online Profile

Now that you have briefly reviewed your basic activities, interests and groups, let's get back to your profile, if nothing else to flick that switch to make you all-round available. Our main focus with this book is to help you be successful online. So, here we go. Let's get you your best possible profile and get into the nitty gritty dos and don'ts!

YOUR PROFILE

THE BARE BASICS: What makes up a profile?

Your profile is very simple when broken down into parts. There are…

THE PICTURE – THE USERNAME - THE HEADLINE – THE DESCRIPTION

After all these, sometimes you will have THE NARROWING OF THE SELECTION POOL then of course… your HAPPILY EVER AFTER (which I'll go into more detail in the next sections)

In most online dating and relationship sites, you will have a basic structure so regardless of which site you choose, these main tips will be relevant and the finer details will most likely be relevant too.

Your profile is your own designated page, which is

essentially you in a nutshell. It contains your username, punch line or headline, photos, description and also what you're looking for in your potential partner. This is your chance to display how amazing you really are (and from the past 21 days, you are oh so ready to put your best self forward!). The profile is so often daunting to many but from your 21 days of self-discovery, your true self should be on the tip of your tongue. Don't forget, online dating is the only way you meet people where you are able to rewrite what you would say about yourself, unlike the mumble and splutter which sometimes comes out when we meet someone we're interested in! So you have a few days to sit down, calmly compose and refine your profile. To have the best outcome from your online relationship experience, you want to project yourself as best as you can. Put that best foot forward and show this pool of people, wanting the exact same thing as you, how great you are. You'll have people contacting you right, left and centre!

The tips below are for all aspects of your profile from choosing the right username to your snazzy one-liner all the way through to your description and of course, your pictures!

TIP 1: BE HONEST

You're only hurting yourself by inflating your profile

So how do you honestly and morally sell yourself & attract the people you want? It's simple! Be you 100%. Think of it this way, the more you inflate your profile or even outright lie, the more stories you will need to remember, not to mention the fact that one day your conscience might get you! However you see this, being truly honest and true to yourself is the best way to be always so stick to this and do the same for your profile. If you are entirely truthful, you can happily and confidently move to the next step and meet someone you've met online. Should you inflate your stories a little, you will end up feeling self-conscious and have self-doubt when heading to the date. You can only hold on to lies for so long, then they'll come back to bite you where it hurts, haunt you and get you into trouble. The truth always unravels the lie and it's not a pretty sight, particularly when the lie is bigger and even more so the longer you have held on to it. If your profile is what-you-see-is-what-you-get, then you can head off to your date knowing that this person has already chosen you, they love your profile, they're already thinking of you as a potential partner.

Besides hurting yourself, by not being truthful in your profile, you're wasting others' time and potentially hurting them too.

Friends are always good to help keep you honest and also help you show your best self. After all, you want to still show the world how great you truly are, you're just being honest, and not over the top.

TIP 2: DON'T OVERSELL!

In fact, slightly undersell :) Leave a little for when you meet in person! It's always refreshing to talk to the person you met online and find out more about them rather than you both simply reciting your profiles again in person.

It's very hard to put who you are into words. Hopefully from doing the worksheets in Part 1, you've been able to see your personality, wants, likes and dislikes in some words. These should help you compile your profile far more easily than simply sitting down and starting from scratch.

On the flip side, if you find it easy to put yourself in to words and you just love writing, most likely you were good at story writing as a kid too so in this case, it's quite hard to not write too excitably! This is the danger zone to look overly confident and cocky or even possibly telling a few fibs, even if they're truthful. Someone like this (even if you're not meaning to be) could really turn a lot of people off and you don't want to miss out on meeting some really great potential partners simply because you wanted to tell everything about you all on the one page.

In the end, no one wants to read a novel. So keep it short and concise but have your flavour and personality shine through. Leave a little for when you meet but entice your potential partner to want to know more about you. Think of a layering technique. It starts with your potential partner first seeing your picture, username and punch line, which first makes him or her want to see the rest of your profile. Then they want to be enticed by a few things they connect with which kicks off him or her wanting to contact you. At this point you share a few more things, then when you meet, a few more things again. You slowly layering their knowledge about you as your own layers peel away.

TIP 3: BE CONFIDENT BUT NOT COCKY

The reason Bjorn and I first spoke was that we each saw a "normal" or "standard" profile. In our case, we had also filled in questionnaires (using eHarmony's relationship matching system) so our profiles weren't as important.

The key is... as with TIP 1, be honest. If you know anything about marketing, you'd be used to selling, promoting and giving the best deal or making your product or service appear as number 1. Whilst this is partly true for you to find your match, you only need to be number 1 for one person, not everyone. You're not applying for a job so you don't need to list all of your achievements or what jobs you have had, what cars you've driven. These things do not define you as a person and are not a solid basis for a long lasting relationship.

For meeting your match, consider this...

Say you are an Olympian (you'd have to be from another country otherwise, most people would probably recognize your face.. so if you were from this country, let's just say you're right at the top of your game). There is no need to say:

I have won 5 gold medals and currently hold 3 x WR, 2 x OR etc. You could say…

I absolutely LOVE to train hard and I do XXX or play XXX. I'm looking for someone who is active and would love to share this part of my life with me.

On that note… If there is something you do i.e. a hobby, sport or interest which takes up a lot of time, I suggest mentioning you spend quite a bit of time in that field.

I wouldn't suggest writing… "You need to be ok with the fact that I love to do XX in my spare time." Rather…

"I would love someone to share this passion with me so my two loves can blend. It would be fantastic if you were interested in this area."

If you want a superficial relationship, write up your credentials, the prizes you've won, the car you drive, what you'll buy for your partner and hey presto, you'll have a few takers… just don't expect it to last very long.

Ultimately, just turn things down a notch if you have the tendency to talk yourself up a little. I like to say, be calmly confident. Know who you are, what you want, what you like to do and how you like to be. Share this and you'll be on the right track.

TIP 4: KEY WORDS NOT TO USE!

YOU NEED, MUST BE/HAVE/WANT – my prospective partner needs to (insert your inflexible need here)

Now we all have things we think are non-negotiables, but it's more in the wording that will either send people running or draw them in. It's not so much what your non-negotiables are, as it is your approach. Sometimes you can simply leave out these particular elements but sometimes they definitely do need to be mentioned, as they really are, 100% non-negotiable. A few of examples in this area would be something like wanting to have children, already having children or being a certain religion. These three key points are ones you need to agree on. They're also usually one of the questions you fill out on your profile so they don't necessarily need to be in your description section. If you're quite passionate in this area, I'd say you would probably want to mention something in your description, as this factor most likely would be a major part of your life.

So, here I am calling them non-negotiables as they won't be changing any time soon and you're very passionate in this area but this still doesn't mean you need to word it aggressively by using the words NEED or MUST and I certainly wouldn't recommend saying "I have these non-negotiables, listed below". All I am saying here is yes, we all have things we're not flexible with (yes, they're non-negotiables), just word it in a softer manner so you don't unnecessarily turn people away.

Instead, turn your non-negotiables into a positive statement. Here are some options to use:

I would love it if you shared...

I am very passionate about…

I have two amazing children and would love you to be involved in their lives. I would also love to also be a part of your children's lives, should you have them. I'm sure my children would love some extra children to play with too. Alternatively, you don't need to have children, just happy to be around my children, as I love them dearly.

I WON'T ACCEPT / TOLERATE

These are simply aggressive expressions. I'm not saying don't say what you want and don't want, just word it appropriately rather than attacking someone you have never met through your aggressive profile. By all means be assertive but just don't attack. This is often a hangover from a past relationship, or at least could be viewed this way. If this aggression is from a past relationship, use these words and feelings in a letter to that person, then burn it (don't send it)!

On most sites, you'll usually find a box that has "DISLIKES" or something similar. Here you're being asked to state what you don't want and you can simply put them in single words, without needing to emotionally describe your hatred for whatever it may be.

So as I said before, if you have a tendency to get a little overexcited, either happily or negatively, just reread what you write and soften it a little. Sometimes your wording could come across far worse than you intended!

TIP 5: STATE WHAT IS DEAREST AND MOST IMPORTANT TO YOU

As I said in Tip 4, this would usually be where you would mention big sticklers i.e. Having children or your faith. Again, perhaps, you meet with your pottery group for 3hrs each night, 3 nights a week or you're training for a triathlon. State what is really important to you and you wouldn't change it for anyone else (just don't say "and I'm not willing to change a thing or be flexible with my time for anyone else". However, these aspects of your life need to be mentioned. They're a part of what you love doing. Sometimes you will be more flexible and other times you won't be. The more specific you are about what activities you do, down to including hours of time taken up, the more likely you are to divide your viewers. This is purely your choice. Sometimes it could be good to weed out the ones not interested in your field and attract the ones who would like to join you. Other times what you do now is purely to fill time which, if you had a partner, you'd be more than happy to be spending all of those hours with him or her. Or you could be somewhere in between? Wherever you are, word this section appropriately. Have a few friends read your profile before posting it and see if they see you have pinpointed where you lie with your passions and how this would affect you and your future relationship.

A successful relationship is one where you actually get to see each other and share some interests together. Without this, you'll live parallel lives. If you're happy with this and your partner is happy with it, then you've stated what you like doing and that's that. You'll sleep in the same bed and you'll have a blissful life together!

It's no good pretending that any relationship has a future if your record collections disagree violently or if your favorite films wouldn't even speak to each other if they met at a party.
-Nick Hornby

Another pointer is your work and sleeping pattern. If you just love early mornings or you're a night owl, this could be something to simply say (not necessarily essential but it helps paint a picture of you) i.e. I'm a night owl and love reading my fantasy books into the wee hours of the morning! Imagine meeting your match who loved doing the same thing?!! Another example could be... I never stop moving, I'm a sun loving, water baby, I love nothing more than to get up just before sunrise to be down on the water on my stand up paddle board, watching the sun rise!

Describing yourself and your life is essential. You will either find people who click straight past you, don't worry, you didn't want to meet them anyway or you will find people who just love and do exactly what you do and how you behave. Alternatively, you will also have people click on you, find you intriguing and it won't bother them what you're activities are and how you behave and they are more than happy to live within and accommodate your life. The key is finding those people and you have the same feeling about their profile and hopefully them when you meet in person.

Remember, you don't need to be clones of each other but it's great if you share a lot of things in common! The main thing is, you don't want to severely dislike things they do. It's best to find someone where you don't mind either way the things they do but you don't do.

TIP 6: DON'T BE NEGATIVE

I know this is a double negative but I really mean this, rather than "BE POSITIVE" which I feel has a totally different meaning. By all means, be this way. These tips are for a successful profile and this tip is a "what to avoid" for success.

We all have things we don't like and don't like in people but there's no need to state this in your profile. See the glass as half full. When you meet with your partner over the next 4-5 dates, your dislikes will come through. Say who and what you are and attract what you want.

E.g. I am truly honest and moral and I feel quite strongly about my values. I would treat you with utmost respect and you will always be my special person whom I'll never aim to hurt.

Rather than...

NO timewasters, NO cheaters, NO bitches... If you think for a second I would put up with this, think again. I hold myself in much higher regard than that!

This may seem extreme, but I have seen it. This wording is aggressive and a big warning sign to stay away from these people. So even if you think it, (of course, no one wants to be treated that way) there's no need to write it. Even if you don't have any hang-ups from your past, it will look this way. Write how you are and attract the same!

TIP 7: LEAVE SOMETHING FOR THE IMAGINATION

As I said before... if you are an Olympian, you like training a lot and competing in X events.

If you've written 5 international bestsellers, you love to write books, it's your hobby, your love, your profession.

If you have the best bum the world has even seen, you do not need to upload a selfie in your lacy French knickers or your CK jocks!

If you are a multimillionaire, that's great, but who are you as a person? You're a driven and motivated person who loves setting big personal goals for yourself.

Statistics and achievements are for getting jobs not partners. Material or aesthetic qualities can be nice bonuses (if that's what you like) but they're the cherry on top, they are not YOU. You are a series of emotions not a collection of objects. All your achievements and material possessions will come out over time as your relationship progresses. We need to get you to this stage first!

TIP 8: YOUR USERNAME AND PROFILE PUNCHLINE

Even though your username is the first thing an online profile will ask for, I have left this until tip 8 only for the fact that you will think on the name for quite a while initially and then change it at the end after you have filled in your profile anyway. Usually, by simply filling out your profile, you'll have some creative usernames and punch lines pop into your head during the process.

So be inventive! Be creative but not so cryptic or obscure that you lose a number of people when viewing your profile. After all, you want people to give you a chance, at least enough to want to click on you to read a little more about you.

For your **username**, what makes you uniquely you?

Do you have a quirky name your friends call you (unrelated to your given name or a pet name from a previous partner)?

What is it that makes you stand out from the crowd?

If the name you want is taken, keep thinking. Making your profile name look like a number plate (because you couldn't get the name in only letters) could seem initially kind of cool but it could give off the wrong vibe or confuse those who aren't used to converting numbers to letters in their head to read your name. Keep it simple, unique and creative. I'm sure you are made up of more than one name! :)

As I will say a number of times, steer away from being too provocative. If you are after love, having a username which is suggestive will give the impression you are more interested in the sex side of things and a long lasting relationship is not as much your priority.

E.g. 1. Couldgoallnight – you could be referring to being a night owl and loving to go out dancing all night however, you could also be suggesting something else; I don't think I need to give details here.

E.g. 2. Sugarpie or cupcake – pet names like this are cute at home once you're in a relationship but when someone doesn't know you, these could seem a bit cheesy or even potentially sexual as porn stars can often choose sweet type names. Save your sweet pet names for once you're in a relationship.

For your **punch line**, create an experience you'd love to share with your partner to be!

E.g. What did you list as your favourite thing to do? Perhaps you could invite them to share your hobby with you?

E.g. 1 – Let's bake triple chocolate cookies together and devour them whilst they're crispy on the outside and hot and gooey on the inside! (you may need to curb this a little for character limitation on your site)

Rather than... I'm a baker and like chocolate.

E.g. 2 – Let's picnic, share a red and the magnificence of the sun's setting

Rather than... I love a good wine.

Set a scene and create somewhere that your potential partner would love to join you.

Most people will describe themselves in a few words and mention what they're looking for in this section so stand out purely by not writing that you're e.g. funny, sweet and looking for someone to share good times. Aren't we all?

Again, avoid being too obscure or so overtly quirky that no one knows what you're talking about. Keep it simple but different and stand out!

Also, a quote from a novel or movie may go over potential partners' heads, even though they may love reading or watching movies. It could possibly be too specific so unless you want someone who is your exact replica and has your identical catalogue of novels and movies, you may miss some really good catches!

TIP 9: STAND OUT BUT STAY TRUE – PARTICULARLY FOR YOUR PHOTOS

It is always good to put a face to the username and even a whole body to the profile!

Put up recent, real photos. It's pretty simple.

If you have photos which really don't look much like you, you have a costume on or they've been retouched or taken by a professional who has made you up to look completely unlike you, leave those pictures for later. You may think these are some of your best photos but do they truly reflect who you are and how you look most of the time?

As I'm sure you also feel, you want to know that what you see in the photos online is what they will look like when you meet them in person.

So your No. 1 picture should be essentially you – no fluff around you, not some crazy occasion, not you in a group or you obviously really partying hard (cut out from the group), it's just you. A nice close-up face shot is great for your profile shot. If you have a full length shot which still clearly shows your face then that's ok too. Go for natural; how you are most of the time, something which reflects your personality as a whole so doing a crazy stunt or looking like a bit of a poser may give off the wrong vibe for the viewers first image of you. If you are truly still at this stage of being fairly superficial, put up your Miss or Mr Poser or your Look-at-me-and-what-I-can-do shot as your number 1 and all supplementary images. Unfortunately, I don't see these exterior-based photos attracting the right kind of potential partner for life-long love and a long-lasting relationship.

For your supplementary pictures, you can have some more activity-based or fun-loving shots but just make sure they aren't your whole album. Ensure you show all sides of you, your quiet and gentle side, your inner child, your daredevil, your Prince Charming or Princess side, your adventurer side, your work side, you all over. Whatever you put up, take your viewer on a visual journey of you in a nutshell, a good reflection of you as a whole and keep all of your photos tasteful e.g. if you have a shot of you bungee jumping and you have only ever done it once, it's probably not the best reflection of you in your everyday life. If, on the other hand, you are after someone to share your adrenalin pumping activities often, then definitely put it up! Certainly don't hide what you love doing in fear of turning someone off. Be raw, open and honest and someone will love all of your photos!

You will most likely have photo tips on whichever site you sign up to but most will tell you not to have photos where you're wearing sunglasses or you're in big crowds (they sometimes require blocking out the other faces). I certainly do not recommend you cutting yourself out of romantic shots. It's still pretty obvious that you're with a past partner in the picture and this could convey that you're still hung up on this person or your relationship has just finished so you have no other photos – either way, fresh out of a relationship can often mean unfinished issues or that the other partner is still hanging around. Regardless of what the photos with previous partners mean to you, try to find ones that don't have you in these situations to save others making assumptions when viewing your profile.

Also, webcam or poor quality shots suggest you can't be bothered taking proper pictures of yourself. Good quality, well-lit photos could make a difference in getting potential partners to click on your profile. Just think to yourself, would I click on that shot?

TIP 10: STEER CLEAR OF BEING SEXUAL OR RAUNCHY

This particularly applies to your pictures as well as what you write. However, as much as we don't like to admit it, people will form their own judgments based on your pictures alone, within the first few seconds of viewing your profile. Of course, when looking for a partner, you want to have some physical attraction but it's not the be all and end all. Being particularly raunchy in your photos could potentially attract the wrong sort of person and get you

in to some trouble and also certainly not attract the relationship type of person you're looking for.

If you're simply after sex, then go for it! If you're after a relationship, it's a given that eventually you'll have sex, you don't need to sell sex to your partner. In fact, I would suggest hiding your sexual assets on your profile... They can be part of your "leave something to the imagination"!

YOUR DESCRIPTION

So you have all of your tips, you're aware of what your profile and supplemental pictures need to look like to attract the right person and you have some ideas for your username and punch line. Now it's time to put your description together.

I like to think in 3 sections.

Remember you want to be brief but enticing.

Lay your description out in 3 paragraphs:

1st paragraph should ideally be about you, who you are and what you like to do. Your first 21 days should make this paragraph a cinch.

2nd paragraph should be about the things which separate you from the rest. What makes you unique or quirky? What are your idiosyncrasies? What are your pet peeves? Remember, write this in an unaggressive manner. ☺ This paragraph would be a section that would either excite people or make them move on. It sorts out your potentials for you.

3rd and final paragraph should be about what you have recently been doing. Think about places you have been, movies you have seen, books you have read. Also think about what you would like to be doing in the future (travelling, reading, studying). This again, will either excite or deter your prospective partners. Remember, don't be shy to say what you want, be unique and specific, as there is someone out there wanting the same or at least similar!! If you don't say it, someone may skip right past you! Stand out and be exclusive. You'll catch the right person's eye!

This should go without saying... but spell and grammar check! Have someone proof your profile for this too! This could be just one of my pet-peeves but if you have major spelling or grammar issues possibly due to being a tad slack, I would dismiss you and potentially miss out on an otherwise amazing catch! An easy way could be to create or copy your profile description into a program with a spellchecker.

Now it's time to put yourself out there! HOW EXCITING!!!

Keep in mind... what you first put up does not have to be the final one, just do your best over the next 4 days. Write.

Review. Improve. Review. Improve. Just put up your A+ version and know that you're giving yourself the best opportunity to meet the perfect person for you. In Part 3, I'll go through ways to analyse your matches and contacts. So without going into all that detail right now, just think and trust your gut. Check out a few of your responses. If you see a pattern of really similar people contacting you, reassess your profile. Perhaps you could reword some of your sentences, be more specific or a little less specific if your pool seems too narrow and not exactly what you want to attract. Then remember that it takes a while to meet people as friends, business partners and certainly finding love... so don't expect love at first click! As you grow as a person in a week, a month, a year, your profile will need to grow with you. You can chop, change, update, delete, improve your profile as many times and as often as you like. Just try to keep some consistency so you are not creating completely different identities (that wouldn't be so cool, and would be completely against the concept showing your true self)!

Which dating site is right for me?

There are so many different sites around the world; I won't be able to list them all. What I would like to do, however, is go over some tips from what I have learnt and also what you can do to learn more and choose the right site to help your online romance bloom.

So to start with, if you are looking for someone in a specific niche, then I can almost guarantee there will be a site out there for you! Gone are the days where online dating had the stigma that it was only for "geeks" or "losers". Nowadays, if you want it, you can get it! You can just Google to find what you're after. e.g. specific same sex sites, religious sites, over 50s sites, hook-up sites and of course all the fetish type sites too. Do the searching yourself and see what you find. Or else, here are some ideas of what to look for and think about... Remember, our focus here is to find love and long term relationships so I'm not covering all the dating sites or what's popular for particular groups of people.

To put it simply, there are two types of dating sites. Long term relationship sites and hook-ups or short fling sites (specific groups will be subsets of these). Some sites will show both types and this is where it gets confusing as you need to decipher this yourself. It is up to you but I would prefer to go to a specific relationship site to narrow the chances of being messed around.

There are a small number of worldwide sites that offer behavioural or personality matching systems. These usually include longer than average questionnaires to learn what you are after. I used eHarmony and found the questionnaire very lengthy. My way of thinking was, if anyone has bothered to go through this process, then they have to be interested in a relationship! As you know by now, it certainly helped me find my one, and relatively quickly (only 2 months!), so as the saying goes... no pain no gain hey? ☺ Was it their matching system that sped up this process? I can't know for sure. My thought is, either way, I was ready to meet my one and their site attracted people of a certain type - those who were ready to be in relationships.

So, my advice to you is... Choose a site which resonates with you. I am not affiliated with any sites and I want you to make your own decisions. Do you want to be sent matches (ie. do the questionnaires and use a scientific algorithmic matching system)? Or are you happy to trawl through profiles on other sites which are relationship based but don't require the lengthy questionnaires to match you? This is your decision. You may even like to try out a few sites and see what kind of response you get. You may see a pattern of people you really like, or definitely not your type at all. Sometimes sites start out with their goal of their target market but their customers start to skew their direction. Follow your heart but keep your head switched on. Find where you feel you belong.

Here are some examples but are certainly not what you are limited to...

Personality or Behavioural matching system sites:

http://www.eharmony.com/

http://www.chemistry.com/

https://www.zoosk.com/

Now, if these sites don't run in your country, have a look around for other sites that offer this type of matching. eHarmony for example runs a little differently to most, where they send you a list of people that could be your possible match each day. If you don't like that round, you wait until the next day. By doing it this way, you actually give time to each person to learn more about them, rather than judging a book by its cover (which you would do by scrolling through profile shots).

Try to steer away from sites like Tinder and Grindr if you are truly looking for love and a long-term relationship. These sites are specifically designed for hook-ups.

Price range could be a factor for you, as sites do vary. There are plenty of free sites, though keep in mind that added perks and a larger membership base may offset this cost. In reality, the minimal cost of any site is incomparable to you finding your one. Paying money to a site should also increase your chances, as only serious people would be doing this. I've found to look at the benefits over the cost works (within reason of course).

How about word-of-mouth? Do you have any friends that have tried online dating with success? Investigate what your friends have found. Listen to what they have to say about their experience with their chosen site.

Security should be another factor to think about. Are you happy to let others search for you and be bombarded with emails? Or would you prefer the type of service I mentioned before - eHarmony? I'm sure there are others that are similar to this, but as it is who I used, I know their process much better than the others. This isn't to say you couldn't find the same elsewhere or better. I haven't focused on giving my opinion on each site as I feel it's a personal decision. How I see a site, will not be how you see it. This approach is how I have worked throughout these first two parts. I want YOU to decide what YOU want and know who YOU are. There is no right or wrong here.

Here are a few larger, or well-known brands going around. See what you think. Again, remember, these sites are simply some examples; you are not limited to this. The world is literally your oyster!

http://www.perfectmatch.com/

http://www.match.com

http://www.date.com

http://www.lavalife.com

http://www.rsvp.com

STEP TWO – ATTRACT THE RIGHT ROMANTIC PARTNER

I'd love to compile your experiences from your relationship sites for where you found true love and your one. I have only listed some examples above based on what I have read and heard from others. As I said, I am not affiliated with any sites and do not have personal experience with multiple sites. I feel the best advice I can give is from you, the ones who have used these sites first hand, from all walks of life.

Please send your feedback on these sites to: datingsitereview@findloveonline.co

Include -

    Name of site

    Cost of membership

    Date and duration on the site

    Usability of site

    A brief description of you and why you felt it was suitable for you

    Who you would recommend this for e.g. age, type of relationship, any specifics

Remember, our focus is finding love and long-term relationships. I would like to keep the review clear and concise so specific niche type dating sites won't be included in this review.

Take a look at our website for a complete list of current reviews at www.findloveonline.co/datingreviews

HOW TO PICK THE RIGHT ONE?

So your profile is up and you've had some matches, connections and even possible emails. Wooohoooo! How exciting!

The question is, how do you really sort through these people and evaluate if they're worth pursuing? How do you know if they're really who they say they are? How do you read their profile and pick if emotionally, they're on the same level as you? How do you continue your layering technique and not jump in to something way too quickly and have repeat failing relationships, often the same as you have had in the past? Most importantly, how do you keep yourself present, not judging people on your past or fretting about your future before it's even started? How do you set some ground rules to stick to your guns, rather than settling for someone who is just ok purely because you want a relationship now? After all, you've waited so long or you've had a relationship you would rather forget, so you want someone in your life ASAP!!

Let's get into it and find your Mr or Mrs Right not just Mr or Mrs You're-OK, with as little messing around as possible!

I said at the end of Part 2, the key to finding the right person is be patient and open minded. Go with the flow and trust your gut. However, you still need to keep your wits about you and also keep your logical brain in gear to prevent you from being swept off your feet by someone who may seem like Mr or Mrs Right at the time, but is so far from it in reality. So we need to find a happy medium, one where there is still romance and excitement but where you also keep your safety and sanity in check too! Remember, you are better to take longer to find the right one and spending time in your "screening" stage than having multiple, less than desirable relationships. Whatever happens along the way, remind yourself that practice makes perfect and everything happens for a reason. So get out there, be in it to win it, be active and practise dating and meeting! The more you do it, the easier it becomes and the more likely you are to meet your one. Being static will certainly not have your one knocking at your door. Being active with people whom you already know are interested in similar things and want to meet you will make it all the more easy!! It doesn't mean they're all perfect for you but it sure makes the dating a lot easier! Get out there and practise and don't give up on Mr or Mrs Right! Analysing and examining each prospective is some of the most exciting times when meeting someone. It allows you to really focus, fine tune, and discover more things about yourself and what you really want out of life (more than you ever even thought about) eventually meeting someone better than you ever thought you wanted! Now, isn't that absolutely tremendously exhilarating!

Last but not least, remember that online dating is not your be all and end all. It is, if nothing else, your catalyst to meet your one. All the effort you put in to your self-discovery and then gaining confidence to first put your profile up is one of the biggest steps to making yourself emotionally available. So keep your eyes peeled wherever you go. You are now exuding confidence and openness, a renewed happiness within, a passion for life and everything you live for and this alone, attracts people wherever you go. New friends. New potential partners.

Now, the next ten tips may seem a little negative but I don't want you going in to the dating scene wearing rose coloured glasses. As fantastic as online dating is, cutting your time easily in half and giving you a far greater, more specific pool, it also can have some downsides. There are a lot of dodgy people out there wanting to make quick money and one of the easiest ways is to appeal to someone's emotions, especially one who has been after love for so long. Someone wanting love so badly, to these people, is like putty in their hands. So I want to make you aware and be able to make educated decisions and not get caught out. You've already had enough of a rough trot trying to find love, the last thing you need or want is someone taking advantage of your generous heart.

So bear with me for these next ten tips, I don't want to pull you down after the first 2 parts have made you feel wonderful and excited. Simply take this information as knowledge to help you find your Mr or Mrs Right, not to deter you from everyone out there or to think everyone is bad. There are so many fantastic people out there waiting to meet you!

One more thing to remember – these tips will go on further than the first 6 days of evaluating your matches. This information can act as a little relationship bible for you, should you feel something isn't right in your relationship. These pointers could help bring clarity to how you are feeling and help lead you in the right direction to either improve your relationship, seek help or simply get right out of there!

Step Three is to simply complete your final days in your 30

day journey. These days will allow you to get in the swing of using your online dating profile, reading and evaluating others' profiles and talking to people. It is after the 30 days where you can sit back and reflect on your past month, see yourself in a new light and see that you're actually thinking about your matches (and potential dates) and reading your emotions for what they are when talking to and meeting people. No more jumping in. You are cool, calm and confident. You go at your own pace and you expect nothing less than to be treated exactly how you want to be treated. You may even like to return to your personal challenge and do the whole 21 days again without talking to anyone (if you really feel you need to let go of more baggage). Otherwise, you could simply continue your daily meditation to help keep yourself grounded and confident whilst chatting to matches and going at your own pace when meeting people.

So, here we go. Let's get the not-so-nice pointers out of the way so you know what to look for and we'll finish with a bang in your BONUS section to help you have an amazing relationship, not just an everyday-existing-together relationship!

TIPS FOR ASSESSING YOUR REPLIES:

TIP 1: How to pick a scammer and liar

I came across Kurt Knutsson one day, who did a great job talking about being baited by catfish on the Dr Phill show. I feel this is a perfect summary of what to watch out for.

Online Dating Scams: How To Tell If You Are Being Baited by a Catfish

It's easy for some of the smartest people to lose all sight of common sense when they're being reeled in by a catfish: an online imposter who tries to win your sympathy - and your love - by creating an elaborate scheme. Award-winning technology reporter Kurt Knutsson, known around the country as Kurt the CyberGuy, shares his top ten reality checks to see if you're being baited by a catfish.

If you identify with at least two of the below scenarios, Knutsson says you could be falling prey to a scam artist.

1. Dumb Date Data

Physical descriptions need to be proportional. For example, someone who is 6-feet tall usually does not weigh 90 lbs. Look for any other descriptions that don't add up to the profile photo.

Tip: Ask them to take a photo holding a unique phrase or their own name on it and send it to you. Ask to have a live video talk using Skype or Facetime. Most of today's smartphones, tablets and laptops come equipped with a built-in camera and/or video. Someone reluctant to speak on live video, claiming shyness or that they can't find a camera, should be a red flag.

2. Profile Picture Test
Professional photos are a red flag. Look for amateur photos — and more than one. Tip: Use a [Google Goggles](#) search on your phone to see if the photo they've shared with you can be spotted elsewhere online. If you see it shown with a watermark or in other settings like modeling websites, it's likely a fake.

3. Become a Photo Detective
"This just takes it to the next level," Knutsson says. Look for detail in photos — wedding rings, locations, activities, time of day, how they are dressed — to see if it matches. Someone claiming that a photo is from a July 4th fireworks party, who is dressed in a fur coat, in daylight, might be a dead giveaway that someone is lying.

Tip: Using a [free inspection service](#) that shows the location and time that a photo was originally taken can shed light on a photo liar.

4. Cut and Paste Profile Alert
Introductory letters on dating websites are often copied by catfish scammers. See if the same information appears in other places or has been copied from someone else by searching for it online. Out-of-country scams often slip up here, revealing inconsistent information such as landmarks and cultural events that don't add up. For example, someone claiming to be from St. Louis who isn't familiar with the iconic Gateway Arch when questioned is likely a liar.

5. Spelling and Grammar Fail
Hear the words when you read their writing, and check their spelling and grammar. A line that sounds like it could be from someone in a far-off country but portraying themselves to be in your same city will usually have a local dialect misfire.

Real: "I just love the Macy's Day Parade in the city."
Foreign Faker: "I just love the Masey's Daytime Parades in the cities."

6. Derailing You from the Dating Site
Red flags should be raised if, right off the bat, they want to get you to instant message or email, taking you off of the dating site where you originally met.

Tip: Always create and use a unique email address that is

7. Too Serious, Too Soon

Watch out for someone rushing things. A catfish usually makes the first move, often out of left field and sometimes creates a bogus, dreamy profile that sounds like the ideal mate you've described in your own dating desires. They play on your sympathy and strike when you are the most vulnerable — caught up in the romance and emotional.

8. Ask a Lot of Questions

Inquire about where they are from, and verify landmarks and spellings of cities online. Blatant errors could mean it's a scam. Catfishers like to ask you a lot of questions, but seldom let you go deep into their lives, coming up with excuses about why they are reluctant to offer more personal information about themselves. For example, they might say, "I've been hurt before by telling too much too soon," which actually turns the tables on you to prove that you can be trusted — Red flag!

9. You Are Not an ATM Machine

If they ask for money, lock them out of your life. Shut off communication immediately, and close all open doors if you have a hint that it is a sympathy scam. Although most catfishers are not after money, this one should be a wake-up call to a scam.

10. Facebook Fakers

At this point, if someone has no Facebook page, but they are sophisticated enough to create an online dating profile, be warned. Also look out for potential fake Facebook pages.

Signs of a fake Facebook profile can include the fact that the Facebook page was started near the same time that a dating profile elsewhere was established, if few photos are posted, or if there are no people tagged in their photos to show a connection in a relationship.

If they are on Twitter, read through historic tweets to see if the story they tell matches up to the same the person you are prospectively dating. Like Facebook, Twitter accounts created around the same time as dating profiles should be treated with caution.

TIP 2: Repeat relationships

The key here is recognizing the pattern. We all find ourselves meeting the same kinds of people from time to time. The way I see it, if you can recognize this pattern sooner each time and change the cycle, you're winning.

Note, that sometimes you can be choosing the same type of person due to something that is going on within you. Sometimes we choose a type because it's an underlying issue we have ourselves e.g. You have anger or internal anger hence you attract an angry person who is aggressive towards you. Other times, we will be attracted to something we subconsciously feel we're lacking (sometimes unknowingly). e.g. If you are very submissive you could attract an aggressive person because you feel unable to express your inner anger. This form of unbalanced relationship can become very toxic and both sides gain no benefit.

The point is, be aware of everything that makes up you and where you are right now. Life is a journey and no one is perfect. The main thing is to attract a person based on your best self and work on your own not-so-desirable parts (hopefully after the previous two parts of this book, you are very aware of you as a whole). Attracting someone based on your own insecurities will always lead to disaster, time and time again. It's time to break this cycle.

There are certain behaviours which most people must avoid.

Physical abuse, that's an obvious one.

Other ones are not so clear so this is where you need to be on the ball.

Verbal abuse – this doesn't have to be a relationship where you're screamed or yelled at. If someone makes you feel inadequate, puts you down, makes snide remarks, puts you down in front of others or makes you feel not your whole self, then these are signs to get out. Your partner should complement you and enhance you, not make you feel worthless or less than you know you are.

I'm not a psychologist and I'm not about to pretend to be one so here's a few links for books I feel are great reads on personalities and behaviours of others. The cost for all 3 books is about $40. If this is an area that interests you I suggest you get all 3!

What Every BODY is Saying
A great book to learn about body language, behaviors and why your brain reacts certain ways.
http://amzn.to/1dTxqdr

I Thought It Was Just Me (but it isn't): Making the Journey from "What Will People Think?" to "I Am Enough"
Brene Brown talks about life as a woman, and how to overcome imperfections in your life.
http://amzn.to/18cldhh

Sway: The Irresistible Pull of Irrational Behavior
An interesting read to open your eyes when making choices in your life.
http://amzn.to/1aEJGGH

Speaking from personal experience, I can relate to one personality trait which I'm sure many of you have come across. This leads me to my next tip – Signs to dodge or fly away. These people woo you in, they're full of life and they appear to have everything going for them!

TIP 3: Signs to dodge or fly away!

Apart from the obvious ones, in this tip, I'm talking about the less than obvious people. The ones who trick you to fall for them, sometimes consciously, but often subconsciously are usually the ones with their own inner demons. Learning to spot this toxic behavior before it hurts you is crucial. If you have unhealthy relationships (romantic or otherwise), you need to assess whether or not these relationships can transform and serve you, or you must find the strength to walk away. After all, you come first!

These types may not be obvious until you have met these people in person however the way they write can often give you some clues too. Simply by being aware of yourself and these types will help you pick it in their writing, however I do like to give someone a chance by at least speaking to them if not meeting them to make sure I do not judge someone simply on their writing style. :)

The Sociopath:

These people are often very vivacious and charming so you get drawn in and fall head over heels very quickly, thinking, "this person has absolutely everything"! Wow, you can't fault them, they've made it in all aspects of life, they're amazing! Within a few weeks, this façade starts to crack and you see these people for who they really are. They have more problems than you! Yes, we all have things we struggle with; we all have talents and are amazing at something. I would go as far to say, there wouldn't be one person in this world who is great at absolutely everything, beautiful inside and out and is charming to boot. So keep your eyes peeled for the "too good to be true" ones. Now, don't get me wrong, when you truly meet your one, you will have similar feelings but they won't jump on top of you all at once! It's a calmer, slower and steadier process. When meeting a sociopath, you can often feel like you're thrown in a washing machine of excitement, lust and activities. After a few weeks, you're absolutely exhausted. How can anyone keep up this pace of passion and action day in and day out??

If you're being accused of something you definitely haven't done, you may have yourself a sociopath or a narcissist! The truth is, your only "fault" was getting involved with one of these types in the first place!

In the case of a sociopath, they'll do everything in their power to make their problems in your relationship be your fault. They will never admit they're lying or wrong. So in this case, simply slide out of the relationship, as quickly and easily as possible, silently repeating to yourself "it's you, not me". After ending a relationship with a sociopath, you could be feeling emotionally very low, diminished and full of despair. This type really crushes your soul and you could end up with a lot of self-blame (when usually in the case of being in a relationship with a sociopath, the problems will have stemmed from their side, rather than your side however much they will tell you it's the other way around). So step back and evaluate the situation. If you can connect your partner to the points below, then it's definitely nothing you have done. Pick yourself back up, dust yourself off and find a person who is just like you and can feel emotions just like you.

I found a great article by Mike Adams, the Health Ranger Editor of NaturalNews.com – I feel he nails the description and identity of a sociopath. I have included only the relevant parts that are most applicable to you and your potential relationship. To view the entire article including videos go to http://bit.ly/192JMbJ.

"How to spot a sociopath - 10 red flags that could save you

from being swept under the influence of a charismatic nut job"

1. Sociopaths are charming

Sociopaths have high charisma and tend to attract a following just because people want to be around them. They have a "glow" about them that attracts people who typically seek guidance or direction. They often appear to be sexy or have a strong sexual attraction. Not all sexy people are sociopaths, obviously, but watch out for over-the-top sexual appetites and weird fetishes.

2. Sociopaths are more spontaneous and intense than other people

They tend to do bizarre, sometimes erratic things that most regular people wouldn't do. They are unbound by normal social contracts. Their behaviour often seems irrational or extremely risky.

3. Sociopaths are incapable of feeling shame, guilt or remorse

Their brains simply lack the circuitry to process such emotions. This allows them to betray people, threaten people or harm people without giving it a second thought. They pursue any action that serves their own self-interest even if it seriously harms others. This is why you will find many very "successful" sociopaths in high levels of government, in any nation.

4. Sociopaths invent outrageous lies about their experiences

They wildly exaggerate things to the point of absurdity, but when they describe it to you in a storytelling format, for some reason it sounds believable at the time.

5. Sociopaths seek to dominate others and "win" at all costs

They hate to lose any argument or fight and will viciously defend their web of lies, even to the point of logical absurdity.

6. Sociopaths tend to be highly intelligent

But they use their brainpower to deceive others rather than empower them. Their high IQs often make them dangerous. This is why many of the best-known serial killers who successfully evaded law enforcement were sociopaths.

7. Sociopaths are incapable of love

They are entirely self-serving. They may feign love or compassion in order to get what they want, but they don't actually FEEL love in the way that you or I do.

8. Sociopaths speak poetically

They are master wordsmiths, able to deliver a running "stream of consciousness" monologue that is both intriguing and hypnotic. They are expert storytellers and even poets.

9. Sociopaths never apologize

They are never wrong. They never feel guilt. They can never apologize. Even if shown proof that they were wrong, they will refuse to apologize and instead go on the attack.

10. Sociopaths are delusional and literally believe that what they say becomes truth, *merely because they say it!*

Charles Manson, the sociopathic murderer, is famous for saying, "I've never killed anyone! I don't need to kill anyone! I THINK it! I have it HERE! (Pointing to his temple.) I don't need to live in this physical realm..."

How to dispel illusion and get to the truth

Sociopaths are masters at weaving elaborate fictional explanations to justify their actions. When caught red-handed, they respond with anger and threats, then weave new fabrications to explain away whatever they were caught doing.

A sociopath caught red-handed with a suitcase full of cash

he just stole, for example, might declare he had actually *rescued* the money from being stolen by someone else, and that he was attempting to find its rightful owner. He's the hero, see? And yet, in reality, he will simply pocket the money and keep it. If you question him about the money, he will attack you for questioning his honesty.

Sociopaths are masters at presenting themselves as heroes with high morals and philosophy, yet underneath it they are the true criminal minds in society who steal, undermine, deceive, and often incite emotional chaos among entire communities. They are masters at turning one group of people against another group while proclaiming themselves to be the one true saviour. Wherever they go, they create strife, argument and hatred, yet they utterly fail to see their own role in creating it. They are delusional at so many levels that their brains defy logical reasoning.

You cannot reason with a sociopath. Attempting to do so only wastes your time and annoys the sociopath.

Tip for exposing sociopaths: Start fact-checking something they claim.

One simple method for dispelling sociopathic delusion is to **start fact checking their claims**. Do any of their claims actually check out? If you start digging, you will usually find a pattern of frequent inconsistencies. Confront the suspected sociopath with an inconsistency and see what happens: **Most sociopaths will become angry or aggressive when their integrity is questioned**, whereas a sane person would simply be happy to help clear up any misinformation or misunderstanding.

Beware of fact-checking the sociopath by asking other people under his or her influence. A sociopath will usually have a small group of cult-like followers who not only believe their fictional tales, but who actually internalize those fictions to the point where they rewrite their own memories to be consistent with them. Fact-checking a sociopath **requires evidence from outside his circle of influence**. Does anything he/she say actually check out in the real world, outside his sphere of direct control? If not, you've probably spotted a sociopath.

Inventing bizarre tales: One of the easiest signs to spot is how sociopaths exaggerate things to an irrational absurdity. In the sociopath's world, every explanation is more intense and more heroic-sounding than the way it really went down. Where a normal person might say, "I vomited last night," a sociopath would say, "I vomited up a 27-foot tapeworm!"

Every story the sociopath weaves, often on the spur of the moment, is impossible to either confirm or deny. No one can prove him or her wrong, since they weren't there, so he or she can spin whatever details into the story he wants.

Kelly O'Brien has some few pointers below to help you spot a narcissist and walk away. Kelly Lynn is a Wellness

Expert at MindBodyGreen, Freelance Writer for multiple publications & magazines.

See the full article here: http://bit.ly/196noS2

6 Qualities of a Narcissist:

1. He or she rarely takes responsibility for problems and instead blames them on everyone else.
2. The narcissist expresses little emotion, particularly during conflict with you. When you do express emotion, he or she blames you for doing so. It's a subtle form of abuse.
3. He or she drains you, but thrives on your energy. Consider how much energy you are expending on this relationship... my guess is that it's your effort keeping the relationship alive. You're most likely exhausted emotionally and physically because you do all of the planning, all of the apologizing, and all of the work to 'fix' what is wrong.
4. This person is charming, often a flirt, and thinks very highly of him or herself.
5. This person is irresponsible with his finances, career, drinking, and/or keeping his home in order.
6. Jekyll & Hyde: This person is so incredibly endearing, but when you say one thing wrong, he or she snaps at you. You walk on eggshells wanting to do everything right.

Once you have determined that you are with a narcissist, the wisest thing to do is to walk away.

Why?

There is no reasoning with this individual. You will inevitably lose every single argument and end most conflicts thinking everything was your fault. You will end up apologizing. You will end up in counseling and you will be the one to end up losing your self-esteem.

You can avoid all of this!

5 Steps to Ending a Relationship with a Narcissist:

1. Distance yourself emotionally and physically from this person

Simply be unavailable, take a step back to get your bearings so you can walk away.

2. Realize that the problem is not you

You need to explore why you attracted this personality type, but that's the *only* place where you need to put your focus. Anything this person said or did to you is their challenge and not a fault of yours. A narcissist will never blame himself.

3. When you are ready which I hope is quickly, walk away

It will be painful but walk anyway, and quickly. Do not argue with them or provide long explanations as they will attempt to bait you into staying. Walk and don't look back. You will be glad you did. If it's a spouse or boyfriend, narcissists move on quickly. Within weeks or a few short months, they will be in love with someone else.

People may wonder how you let such a "charmer" get away. Stay true to yourself and do NOT worry about what others think. Trust that any intelligent person will go through the same situation and will walk as well.

4. Free yourself from needing others approval

Often, people who need approval are the ones who attract this abusive personality type. Do not look to another person for 'approval' because you will never feel fulfilled. If you look to a narcissist for approval? You will fall into feeling completely abused and you will regret.

5. Love yourself and surround yourself with people who genuinely love you

Here is a definition of Narcissistic Personality Disorder from the Psych Central:

Symptoms of Narcissistic Personality Disorder

In order for a person to be diagnosed with narcissistic personality disorder (NPD) they must meet five or more of the following symptoms:

Has a grandiose sense of self-importance (e.g., exaggerates achievements and talents, expects to be recognized as superior without commensurate achievements)

Is preoccupied with fantasies of unlimited success, power, brilliance, beauty, or ideal love

Believes that he or she is "special" and unique and can only be understood by, or should associate with, other special or high-status people (or institutions)

Requires excessive admiration

Has a very strong sense of entitlement, e.g., unreasonable expectations of especially favorable treatment or automatic compliance with his or her expectations

Is exploitative of others, e.g., takes advantage of others to achieve his or her own ends

Lacks empathy, e.g., is unwilling to recognize or identify with the feelings and needs of others

Is often envious of others or believes that others are

envious of him or her

Regularly shows arrogant, haughty behaviours or attitudes

Now, as I said, I'm definitely not psychologist or psychiatrist hence why I have included these guests' defining points. I feel it's good to have a base knowledge of particular behavioural patterns that you could easily come in to contact with so that when you meet someone you're aware. This is not to say that there is something wrong with everyone. It is simply to be aware and for you to decide if you are happy in a relationship with one of these types.

As I said before, there are a few behavioural patterns which I would say most people would prefer to steer away from for their own self-preservation and for a long lasting, equal and loving relationship. Some of these disorders (or I would prefer to call them behaviours) do not suit relationships, as we know them i.e. equal love with even give and take – the fairy-tale. Once you have identified who you are, what you want in your life, you'll know what you're happy to attract (and of course, by simply being, you'll attract your similar type to suit you). There are people who like to help and serve – so perhaps for these people being with people with these disorders, you could call them an "opposites attract relationship". However, often in this case, you could be fighting an uphill battle and possibly never have a solution or a positive outcome, at least not the one that you're hoping will eventuate.

For a "like attracts like" relationship – If you are a sociopath and you don't wish to change, then finding another sociopath could work for you. You two could simply live completely parallel lives under the one roof whilst going to big events and parties as a couple. I see this as a fairly superficial relationship and certainly not love but as we have now attained, sociopaths and narcissists are incapable of loving others and are more self-absorbed so a relationship of this kind could be a great way to go! This would also prevent other people who want true love being hurt by keeping like with like.

TIP 4: Learn from your mistakes

So, you've caught yourself in these awful relationships, realized what's going on and you're out! We have all had things happen to us that aren't ideal. It is how you deal with them and what you choose to do with these experiences that will influence your behaviour in your new relationship and ultimately help you have a happier, longer lasting existence with your partner.

So learn what you do and don't want in your partner. Of course, if you have a checklist based on material things, as I've said before, you're most likely not going to get a deep and meaningful relationship. Once you know yourself and you've had a few partners (if you haven't been lucky enough to snag your perfect match first time around), you'll start to collect a mental list of the type of person who matches you (as well as knowing what doesn't work with you). It's not always as black and white as this. I would like to add one more dimension to your likes/dislikes. It's what doesn't bother you, the area where you are flexible and accommodating. You do not need to meet the perfect person. An amazing relationship to me is one in which you share your big likes, you accept the bits that your partner feels are non negotiable but you're happy to support or be flexible in all other areas and vice versa.

TIP 5: Your scars and your partner

You've started dating or you're in a fresh relationship... Be aware that your new partner has not had your experiences and they are certainly not your past partners!

If you find yourself starting to accuse or blame your partner on something that is your own insecurity from other relationships, pull yourself up. Go back through your initial 21 days. Remind yourself of your amazing qualities and practice your meditation and relaxation techniques to bring you back to the present moment. Remember, your past happened for a reason, to teach you lessons and to be a stronger person however, you are not defined by your past or past relationships. Leave them in the past where they belong and focus on being the best person you can be, be stronger, be your true self. Be in the best relationship you can be in and always give your partner the love and trust they deserve.

If your past is still haunting you and your irrational behavior towards your partner continues however much you truly love this new person in your life, seek some help if you can't deal with your issues alone. Wouldn't you prefer to face these issues head on (regardless of how hard it is) if it would help you keep this amazing person in your life?

TIP 6: It's just not going to work

Part I – The emotionally unavailable:

You need to both want the same thing. Perhaps, being online helps identify who is ready and not ready for a relationship. There are some sites more aimed at a singles market, wanting simple flings whereas sites like eHarmony are really aimed towards people wanting to find the ONE.

Be honest with yourself. Do you really match well or do you really just want someone and you want it now? If everything is great from your side, then assess that your partner feels the same.

Signs of an emotionally unavailable person:

- Can't commit
- Can't or won't discuss feelings
- Leaves you always waiting
- Make excuses or is indecisive
- Serial dater
- Won't make long term plans
- Often talk about their past – in particular ex's
- You're doing all the work in the relationship even when you have the same likes and dislikes – the emotional stuff

Signs of an emotionally available person:

- They follow through with promises
- They're contactable
- Talk about the future and make plans
- Discuss feelings and fears
- They're supportive and "show up" for you

To work with someone who truly has issues letting people in (and isn't simply selfish)

Give them 'me' time

Allow them to have separate friendships and time with these friends

Don't push or pressure them

Part II – The expired relationship:

So this could be a little further down the track than just from your initial meeting however, it is still good to know at any point when your time together has expired, be it long or short. The purpose of your whole journey here is to find love, not a mediocre existence together. So the initially painful part will be better for the two of you in the end, when you meet your final ONE!

Below are some relevant points by John Kim, author of When & How to let go of an expired relationship. More detail can be found at http://bit.ly/1l5JbeR

There's no right way to get through a breakup. Each is different, and the amount of time it takes to get over someone can vary. What's important is that you start the process.

Here are a few tips.

1. Know that the relationship has expired.

Yes, like milk there was an expiration date. Know that it was meant to go as long as it did, not one day less or one day more. And you were meant to learn something from it. You'll ask yourself a lot of why questions, like, "Well then does that mean every relationship has an expiration date?" Don't open that bag. The more you believe it was meant to expire, the more you'll be able to let go.

2. Fully feel it.

You can't heal if you're in denial, and not wanting to feel something is a form of denial. You're going through a loss. It meant something. It was a part of your life. Don't deny it or minimize it. Accept it. Fully. I'm not saying lock yourself in your room and replay old songs, but you must allow yourself to feel the pain. Take a day or three and be sad. You invested your heart in this. It deserves to be felt.

Learn from the experience.

There are gifts in every expired relationship. They're called lessons. These lessons will be the branches that pull you out of your quicksand. Although extremely painful, what's produced from your collision are diamonds, revelations about yourself, other people, relationships and the world. This is extremely valuable.

If you don't choose to look at it, take it, embrace it, you're throwing away something that can't be replaced. It's difficult to see what you've learned about yourself after a relationship is over. It's difficult to examine your contribution to why it expired. This requires taking responsibility, and many refuse to do that. But it's also the beginning of the growth process. The more diamonds (revelations) you collect, the more valuable this expiration becomes and the more you realize it was meant to expire. The more of this and the easier it will be to accept and let go.

Remember why it didn't work.

Drill this into your head. When we look back on relationships, we usually play the highlight reel. We play back all the good stuff, the moments when we felt alive and in love and thought it would last forever. We must hit stop and go to the behind the scenes, the fights, the silences, the tears, the abuse, all the reasons why it did not work. If you keep playing the highlight reel, you'll second guess everything and want something that isn't reality. This desire is the quicksand I referred to above. It will keep you stuck and sinking. It didn't work for a reason. That's the focus. Stay there. Replace your emotional thoughts with facts.

3. Get physical.

Get physical with yourself. No, not like that. What I mean

is exercise. It's the best way to release stress. Take your pent up energy and use it to look better naked. Now's the time to do everything you've wanted to try: rock climbing, CrossFit, spin, yoga. If you can't give your mind a rebirth, give your body one and your mind will follow.

4. Turn it into action.

When we think of letting go, we usually focus on the mental or emotional aspect of it. This will keep you in your head. Instead, focus on what it looks like in action. Ask yourself, "What does letting go look like in everyday life?" Picture it. What do you see? Let's say you see yourself working on *you*. Okay, how?

Therapy or self-help

Fitness

Nutrition

Friends

Hobbies

Career

Now break down how you're going to accomplish that in each category.

TIP 7: Criticism: reflection of the critic

From evaluating your behaviours in relation to TIP 5, you also may have come up with some things you are doing which are not actually related to your potential partner nor are they related to past relationships. When you find yourself criticizing your partner, or anyone for that matter, ask yourself, why you are doing it? Are you blaming others for your insecurities? Are you criticizing them and hiding behind your nasty words? Like TIP 5, take a step back, evaluate and amend. Go back through your 21-day journey. After all, we spent 3 full weeks on you for a reason! 21 days to form new habits and beliefs – your new found true, amazing self. So no more critical living! This way of living is only hurting you. You are missing out on this gift of life we have been given! Seek help if you need to talk your problems through, find meditation or yoga and find space to have clarity and free yourself of self-criticism.

TIP 8: A toxic relationship

Toxic relationships are extremely draining. It is very easy to determine when or if you are in a relationship with a toxic person. These people are energy vampires. They constantly push you down and deplete you. A healthy relationship should make you feel enlivened, uplifted and enriched.

In the beginning, it's highly unlikely you'll see the negative side of a person. It's usually as you start to become more familiar with each other, more comfortable, that your not-so-nice sides come out. Of course, we all have our bad days. What you need to look out for is the time in the relationship where your partner never seems to have a good day and they're always taking it out on you (not necessarily angrily, it can be subtle too). When you notice that you feel absolutely exhausted, trying to constantly please your partner then make the decision if you need to address the relationship dynamics or simply walk away. This is your decision and only you know if your connection with each other and your energy is worth it. There are a number of reasons why someone may not be treating you properly. If there are genuine, current things going on which you know will change, then, of course, stick around. I'm not talking about the occasional hiccough in a person's life or a relationship. I'm talking about the constant draining relationship. This is what's toxic. It is ongoing and you can't see a light at the end of the tunnel. The person you are with is set in this pattern and you are feeling very uninspired by this relationship.

So here are some pointers for you to check off and deal with your toxic relationship:

YOU COME FIRST – Know that no one can make you feel a certain way. You choose to respond to their actions and behaviours. Your thoughts create your reality. This is the first point where you know if you want to work through their issues together or walk away when a time feels right for you.

LOVE AND BE HAPPY – Toxic people are this way for a reason. They need love and support but this does not mean YOU need to do this job. By simply being you, your happy confident self, you will rub off on this person. If this relationship has dampened your passion for life too much, then put yourself first, protect yourself. Find your happiness again. You decide if you need to be apart to do this or not. Your partner may feel it's appropriate that they seek help to deal with their issues. In this case, life together may be better and you'll quickly find your happiness. Obviously this would be the ultimate outcome but this isn't always how it works. If your partner doesn't think there is anything wrong with their behavior, then walking away may be the best option for you.

BOUNDARIES – Create your own space for you. By taking care of yourself, your relationship will sort itself out. So, if your relationship and partner are getting you down, set your own boundaries. Either your partner will recognize your change and want to change him or herself or you will have created the space to allow you to walk away.

LEARN – Learn from your relationship. Has this person come into your life for a reason? What have they taught you? Did they bring out a part of you which you want to address? Were you able to help them in some way? Every relationship is different but everything certainly happens for a reason so be the relationship long or short, there was something in it which you needed to learn.

TIP 9: How to say no to a second date

Here is a great article by Alexandra Franzen. She has put together a script for you so you have something to say when you don't want to go on a second date. Of course we will meet people and there just simply won't be any chemistry. It is in this case where you don't want to waste anyone's time and you're best to be honest so you can both move on. If you can do this well, you will find you could make some great friends out of it too! I, personally have met people online, chatted and they seemed great then when meeting in person, we've been honest and said there was no chemistry and we have now been friends for almost a decade! We still laugh about our encounter. So dates, being not what you're expecting them to be, no longer need to be awkward and horrible. There's no need to run for the hills and hide, you have a script here to help you compose your own wording to allow you to not fear these dates and to make something positive from them and if not positive, at least not hurt anyone.

If you're saying, "No, thanks," be exceptionally clear and extraordinarily kind.

If you feel it is too difficult to gently say "no thanks", try something like this:

Hey { name },

I had an excellent time meeting you, and I'm completely intrigued by your passion for {competitive skiing / collecting toy robots / perfecting the art of the grilled cheese sandwich / insert something they talked a lot about, here}.

Thanks for recommending that I check out { name of band / documentary / radio show / book / insert something they mentioned, here }. It's on my Official List of Cool Things To Do and Try as of ... now.

I'll hop straight to it: I think you're terrific — like coconut-ice-cream-with-salted-caramel-on-top-terrific — but I'm not feeling the particular flavor of chemistry that I'm searching for, in a { girlfriend / boyfriend }. I hope we're on the same page. And if not, I hope you understand.

If our paths cross again, I'll be expecting a full update on { your downhill skiing adventures / your ever-growing toy robot collection / that lifelong grilled cheese project }.

Be well,
{ your name here }

The big, golden key?

When it comes to the amount of compassion and love in the universe, you always <u>want to be an Adder</u>, not a Subtractor.

TIP 10: Be 100% happy

Now, I need to add this tip in here. We've had some not so nice tips in this section so I want to finish on a high and have you excited to meet your ONE! Remember, you are after love. You want to find your one. This final relationship is for a lifetime. If you are dating someone initially and you already have doubts, then they aren't the one. There are a few exceptions. The main one is if your potential partner simply isn't opening up to you as quickly as you would like. If this is the case, take it slowly. As long as what you are seeing is positive and what your gut is telling you, of what's lying beneath their layers, is good, then that's OK. Be gentle and calm and they'll slowly open up to you. The closer you get, the easier it will be to talk about more sensitive subjects and the more comfortable they will be to open up to you. Please don't confuse this with someone hiding things from you or being secretive in their behaviour.

Remember, the main thing is, your gut should only tell you good things. Don't make excuses for someone's behavior or tell yourself that you think or feel, "it will get better". Alternatively don't think, "you're being too picky", unless you really are or being like Tip 7 and criticizing everyone who comes your way due to your own self-criticism. It's good to be picky and go after your true match. If you're dating someone and making excuses for them or the relationship, it's not going to improve, in fact, it will get worse the more "comfortable" the relationship becomes. If you want love that will last a lifetime, go for gold! Only settle for someone who gives you butterflies and then your logical brain matches your emotions. For a relationship to last the test of time, your honeymoon phase and the next, at least year of dating, needs to be amazing. You need to feel like peas in a pod, you don't like having time apart, even though you know time apart is good for you! If you truly want to go for what you know you deserve, be patient and only settle for the best. Don't simply settle for near enough because you've waited so long and you just want it all to happen NOW! I'm sure you could have a good relationship for some time, even a lifetime with someone who is ok-enough but you might miss out on the amazing life with someone who could be waiting around the corner for you!

STEP THREE – HOW TO PICK THE RIGHT ONE?

So remember, these 6 days are about practising your romance detective skills. Take your time reading profiles and talking to potential partners. Sit back and do your best to not be too emotionally involved instantly. Be a wary detective. The right person will wait for you and will most likely be doing the same to you. Be careful. Stay true to yourself and your values. Know that the person who you decide is worthy of your heart is the luckiest person in the world, so will be happy to be patient whilst getting to know you!

I'm keen to hear how you go. Should you meet your one, please email me at success@findloveonline.co or else post to our Facebook page at https://www.facebook.com/findloveonline.co. Of course include photos ☺

Oh, and DON'T FORGET ABOUT YOUR BONUS SECTION ATTACHED! How to keep your romance absolutely alive and amazing! The secret to LIVING rather than EXISTING with your chosen ONE!

KEEPING THE ROMANCE ALIVE

Now for the fun part! This chapter is good to know prior to starting a relationship. It will allow you to keep the romance alive once the honeymoon phase starts to wear off! It is also great, even in the beginning, as it can give you some ideas for you to simply do on your own or on dates.

Get out there and live! Don't just exist!

TIP 1: Date nights

If you can't do something special with each other every day, make it once a week! If you can't do it once a week aim to at least do one thing, just the two of you once a month!

This is so important! It is so easy to simply fall into everyday patterns and life becomes dull. It would be the same level of dull if you were alone or with this person. So once the honeymoon phase is over, start adding in the occasional thing you know you both love doing!

BONUS – KEEPING THE ROMANCE ALIVE

List 5 things you know you both love doing (it doesn't need to cost a cent!) e.g. picnic overlooking the ocean, go out dancing on a "school night".

What 5 things do you both love doing together?

1) _____

2) _____

3) _____

4) _____

5) _____

Brigitte Mienders has put together a great list in 7 Habits To Turn A Boring Life Into An Extraordinary One. You can do this for yourself every day and also incorporate your partner whenever you both can!

1. Get up an hour earlier than usual.

Use the time to do some gentle yoga poses, take a walk, or slowly ease into the day instead of frantically running into the shower, driving, or walking to the office, and sitting at your desk before your body has even had enough time to adjust to the new day. It sets the tone for a mellower, happier day.

2. Make a to-do list in the morning.

Make it attainable and realistic and you'll feel good at the end of the day seeing all those check marks.

3. Make movement non-negotiable.

Halfway through your morning and through the afternoon, make a point to stand up and walk around. Walk around your office, take a stroll down the block, whatever you have time for. Do this as often as possible.

4. At lunch, turn away from your computer and focus on your food.

Be in the moment. Get outside if you have time and walk,

read a book, or just take in the day for whatever amount of time you have.

5. Do something different each evening after work.

Don't make a routine out of coming home, eating dinner, and sitting on the couch. My husband and I like to mix things up by going on hikes with our dogs, visiting the beach, going to the movies, out with friends, or having bonfires in the backyard. Just because it is a "school night" doesn't mean you can't enjoy it!

6. Don't get into an eating rut.

Have something healthy that you REALLY enjoy for each meal – perhaps a tasty smoothie for breakfast, delicious leftovers for lunch, and plan a fun dinner – fun to both make and eat! Once you start experimenting in the kitchen, it's hard to stop and the possibilities are endless.

7. Before you go to bed, rehash your day and find gratitude for everything that happened to you that day.

Be thankful.

The most important part of all of this is to practice mindfulness throughout your day. Even on your way to work, which may seem like the most mundane thing ever, take in the weather, the sounds, the sights. At work, notice the people around you, and make the best of whatever your job might be. You're there, so may as well make the best of it and take pride in your accomplishments. Our world is always changing, every second of every hour, so make sure you witness as much of it as you can.

TIP 2: Communication

This is the most important thing in a relationship! TALK... Simply tell each other what you're doing, need to do or would like to do, individually or together. I even suggest sharing a calendar (either online or a hardcopy) so you know what's going on, not to keep tabs on each other, just to be able to consider one another.

Also, simply tell each other what you like and dislike... If you don't talk, how is the other expected to know?

The more open you are, the easier life flows, there is no confusion and you / your partner won't seem deceitful by keep things to themselves.

Get to know your partner and how they work. We all have our idiosyncrasies and if we want to work together as a team for a lifetime, we need to understand and accept how the other works.

If you are looking for a fantastic course to enhance your communication skills together, try Tony Robbins – Date with Destiny. This will change the way you communicate with each other forever!

TIP 3: Honesty and Openness

I feel this is an obvious one but it is still worth mentioning. Be honest. Here is an area, where I know in my relationship and close friends of ours, men and women see honesty and detail as two separate things. The female in the relationship always seems to want to plan more and give ALL of the information to the male – honesty and detail ARE the same thing to the female, you tell the whole truth. The female tends to be more detail focused. On the flip side, the male often will feel they are being completely honest (and they definitely are) but don't give any detail, just the simple facts. The female can often see this as not-the-whole-story and whatever the situation can be frustrated by this, not in necessarily a trust sense, just a lack of detail sense. The male sees honesty as fact and detail is extra information that is irrelevant (to them, but not the female). This comes back to the previous key tip in life-long relationships... COMMUNICATION and understanding how the other works.

I don't think I really need to mention this here but should you be unfaithful or deceitful, expect your relationship to fall apart or at least be far less than what it could have been, had you not done it. Once trust has been broken, your relationship will not be the same again. So start strong and stay strong. Be committed, honest and open and you have absolutely nothing to worry about, except for organizing the occasional thing to make your partner feel special from time to time, or a date night!

Once you're in a permanent relationship, things like passwords, phone locks, computer locks etc., don't necessarily need to be handed over in a handbook to your partner but I don't feel they need to be secret. I go as far to have all my passwords known by my husband just in case I am unable to access something if I'm away or something and he can do it for me. It's entirely up to you what you do with your passwords and locks but just ask yourself a question, "Am I not giving these passwords over because I have something to hide?" If so, address what you're hiding and if it's disastrous, once again, don't expect to have the amazing life you could have! Openness is freedom and happiness. If you are forever haunted by secrets and dishonesty, your physical and emotional health will certainly suffer, along with your relationship.

TIP 4: Eliminate what you both dislike doing

There are things in life which need to be done and you both dislike doing them e.g. washing, ironing, dishwashing and the like. If you can afford it, have someone do this for you (whatever your "dislike" may be). If not…

TIP 5: Make it fair

Share the load in the running of your life. Work out what you both see as a fair deal so one doesn't feel they're doing more for the other. When one feels as though he or she is the victim, the relationship starts to fall apart.

So make it fair, trade what you dislike for something they dislike, but you don't mind doing. E.g. I don't like touching raw meat so Bjorn cuts up all of our raw meat and I wash up more. Bjorn prefers to clean the outside of the house when we have visitors coming over and I do the bathrooms more.

If you both don't like doing the same thing, then set a time in your diary when you both attack it together and get it out of the way! Then reward yourself and go out and do something you both love doing e.g. An extra long jog with your dog or sit down with a satisfying glass of red!

TIP 6: Five Positives for one negative

In all aspects of your life, in dates and your relationship, implement a rule for yourself that your approach to life will always be 5:1 – 5 positive emotions / actions for 1 negative. If you work hard to make this happen, it will be virtually impossible to live in a dysfunctional relationship. If you are in a content or happy state, then the little things don't bother you; they just flow on by. This approach to life will then reflect in your relationship. Your partner's idiosyncrasies won't start to get on your nerves, they will stay on the endearing side and you'll have a positive life together. You will want to spend those special moments together, creating a life with a string of awesome experiences!

About Us

Fi and Bjorn met on eHarmony in February, 2011.. they chatted, they dated, they travelled extensively and then on Fi's birthday in 2012, Bjorn popped the question! They wed 20.12.2012 and decided to spread the word on how to find love online and live an happy and fulfilled life.

It wasn't always smooth sailing for Fi and Bjorn, they have both had relationships fail and dates not be so good, after all, they are in their mid-30s. Learn from those who have been in the same situation as you!

Below is a little about Fi and Bjorn's background...

Fiona Caddies

Fi is an entrepreneur, speaker, author and leader in fitness, yoga, lifestyle and nutrition coaching. She has run multiple personal training businesses, fitness studios and now devotes most of her time to online health and fitness at http://whitezebra.com. Fi believes in really living life over simply existing. Eat and move to nourish the body, be surrounded by those who nourish the soul, do something each day which makes you happy and always believe that something great is going to happen.

Email: info@fionacaddies.com

"Looking good and feeling great is not about diets or restriction, it's about knowing how to think, what to eat, and how to train. Treat yourself well and the rest of life with fall into place."

Bjorn Miller

Bjorn is an entrepreneur, speaker, author and leader in IT solutions. He has worked for multiple large multi-nationals, spoken at large conferences and is a visionary for start-ups and angel investing. Bjorn is the ultimate S.N.A.G (Sensitive New Age Guy).
He too, likes to aim high, dream big, make things happen, drink green smoothies, train hard in and outside of the gym and do yoga too!

Email: info@bjornmiller.com

"Changing the world, one website at a time"

Contact

Sign up for our free newsletters at findloveonline.co

For anything general, please contact:

Web: http://www.findloveonline.co

Email: info@findloveonline.co

Facebook: https://facebook.com/findloveonline.co

We love feedback!

It's how we can improve and continue to help you!

Please give us feedback at:

feedback@findloveonline.co

Before you ask any questions, please see our FAQs first, then ask away at:

questions@findloveonline.co

CONTACT

We also LOVE to hear how you have gone!

Have you grown as a person?

Have you found your one?

For any kind of SUCCESS or GROWTH please contact us at:

success@findloveonline.co

Oh and we love interacting with you on social media!

Please find us at:

Facebook.com/findloveonline.co

Twitter.com/twopeasinpod

Pinterest.com/fiandbjorn

Lastly... Dissatisfied? WE HOPE NOT!

We truly hope you are 100% happy and inspired by our book and our services but should you have any complaints please contact us at: complaints@findloveonline.co

We also recommend you repeat your personal journey (as many times as you like, for itself, independent of relationships) and reevaluate your profile from time to time to fine tune and update it so you can continue to attract the right life partner for you.

FIND LOVE ONLINE

Be patient and see your life as a positive, amazing journey. Experience gratitude in all aspects of your life and see your life change for the better! You read this book for a reason; it was part of the life journey you were meant to take and as we hope, it has had a positive effect on you.

Yours in gratitude

Fi and Bjorn

References

Maraboli, Steve 2013, Unapologetically You: Reflections on Life and the Human Experience

Aristotle's Rhetoric. Available from: <http://rhetoric.eserver.org/aristotle/rhet1-11.html>. [1 November 2013].

Canfield, Jack, Hansen, Mark Victor and Kirberger, Kimberly 2012, Chicken Soup For The Teenage Soul: 101 Stories Of Life, Love And Learning

Whittaker, S. 12 May 2007, Secret attraction, The Montreal Gazette.

Redden, Guy, Magic Happens: A New Age Metaphysical Mystery Tour, Journal of Australian Studies: 101.

The Law of Attraction: Real-Life Stories - Oprah.com. 27 June 2008. Available from: <http://www.oprah.com/spirit/The-Law-of-Attraction-Real-Life-Stories_1>. [12 September 2013].

"Go Beyond 'The Secret' - Oprah.com". 14 March 2008. Available from: <http://www.oprah.com/spirit/Go-Beyond-The-Secret_1/ >. [14 September 2013].

30 things to do before you die. 12 July 2013. Available

from: <http://www.mindbodygreen.com/0-10247/30-things-to-do-before-you-die.html>. [16 September 2013].

Online Dating Scams: How To Tell If You Are Being Baited by a Catfish. Available from: <http://www.drphil.com/articles/article/726>. [20 September 2013].

How to Spot A Narcissist and Walk Away. 27 November 2012. Available from <http://www.mindbodygreen.com/0-6921/How-to-Spot-A-Narcissist-and-Walk-Away.html>. [20 July 2013].

How to spot a sociopath - 10 red flags that could save you from being swept under the influence of a charismatic nut job. 8 June 2012. Available from: <http://www.naturalnews.com/036112_sociopaths_cults_influence.html>. [6 July 2013].

How To Say No To A Second Date (And Still Make Everyone Feel Great). 10 July 2013. Available from: <http://www.mindbodygreen.com/0-10237/how-to-say-no-to-a-second-date-and-still-make-everyone-feel-great.html>. [26 July 2013].

Narcissistic Personality Disorder Symptoms. Available from: <http://psychcentral.com/disorders/narcissistic-personality-disorder-symptoms/>. <10 September 2013>.

When & How to let go of an expired relationship. 7 July 2013. Available from <http://www.mindbodygreen.com/0-10180/how-to-let-go-of-an-expired-relationship.html>. [14 July 2013]

Notes

NOTES

www.ingramcontent.com/pod-product-compliance
Lightning Source LLC
LaVergne TN
LVHW051520070426
835507LV00023B/3209